CW01457456

It's All
About Me

It's All About Me

Alison Kentish

The Book Guild Ltd

First published in Great Britain in 2021 by
The Book Guild Ltd
9 Priory Business Park
Wistow Road, Kibworth
Leicestershire, LE8 0RX
Freephone: 0800 999 2982
www.bookguild.co.uk
Email: info@bookguild.co.uk
Twitter: @bookguild

Copyright © 2021 Alison Kentish

The right of Alison Kentish to be identified as the author of this
work has been asserted by her in accordance with the
Copyright, Design and Patents Act 1988.

All rights reserved. No part of this publication may be
reproduced, transmitted, or stored in a retrieval system, in any form or by any means,
without permission in writing from the publisher, nor be otherwise circulated in
any form of binding or cover other than that in which it is published and without
a similar condition being imposed on the subsequent purchaser.

This work is entirely fictitious and bears no resemblance to any persons living or dead.

Typeset in 11pt Minion Pro

Printed and bound in the UK by TJ Books LTD, Padstow, Cornwall

ISBN 978 1913551 872

British Library Cataloguing in Publication Data.
A catalogue record for this book is available from the British Library.

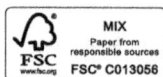

MIX
Paper from
responsible sources
FSC
www.fsc.org
FSC® C013056

For Darren
For putting up with my equine obsession, for never
mentioning the fact that his wife looks and smells like
she lives in a stable most of the time, nor questioning
just how many rugs does one horse need.

For Bond
Obviously
Because it really is all about him.

Introduction to Horses

Apologies to those with detailed horsey knowledge already; I hate to teach a grandmother to suck eggs. (What does that even mean? Why do they suck eggs? That's disgusting! Someone should be teaching them to stick to sucking Werthers.) But for those who need a little introduction to my world, here's some highly accurate and completely unbiased information on a few matters equestrian...

Horses and Ponies

Ponies are just small horses, usually hairier, often more cunning. I'm pretty sure it has been scientifically proven that, for a rider, the closer to the ground you start – by riding a smaller pony – the more likely you will end up face-planted into aforementioned ground.

Horses and ponies are generally regarded by non-horsey folk as big, dangerous, stupid, expensive animals.

But as a distinctly (and often distinctly stinky) horsey person, with many years' experience, I can tell you now, that is completely true.

What is *not* true is that they are all owned by upper-class, rich, champagne-swilling gentry who cavort about the countryside on their steeds before flinging the reins of said steed at one of their humble servants and then going off for a romp in the hay. Would that this were true!

The majority of horses and ponies are owned by hard-working, hard-up, hardy folk who are generally broken, exhausted and penniless from the sheer effort of keeping their beloved equine healthy and happy, never mind ridden or, heaven forbid, competitive.

So why do we do it?

Well, why do people have children?

Seriously. Why? I've often wondered.

It is no coincidence that many horsey ladies I know have chosen not to have children, recognising that they too could be dangerous, stupid and expensive – and they get big too! And if you're not careful they want ponies of their own. Cue even more danger and expense.

But, just as most "normal" people couldn't imagine not having their beautiful, loving children, us horsey folk feel the same about our "babies", and so, just as many parents do, we excuse our "little one's" naughtiness, we ignore the inconvenience, we gloss over the expense and all the compromises and sacrifices we have to make for them, because we love the very bones of them, unconditionally.

Because once you get past the dangerous, stupid and expensive bit, they are incredible. They are generally kind, gentle and loving; they have such characters; they are generous and forgiving; they allow us to do all sorts of things, like riding them and putting them in horseboxes, which go against their natural instincts, because they put their trust in us instead of using their size and strength against us. We get to do amazing things with them, from relaxing on hacks around beautiful countryside to exulting in the thrill of roaring round a course of cross-country jumps. They are humbling to spend time with; I feel honoured to be accepted by them.

Oh, but, man, they are still really very stupid sometimes.

Windy days are scary for them. They often play up when it's cold. They have an amazing and expensive capacity for self-harming. For half-tonne animals, they break incredibly easily. They are destructive (eating fences and stables and trees, ripping their rugs, breaking buckets or frankly anything left alone in the stable with them for five minutes). They are scared of shadows on the ground. They are scared of puddles. And drains. And white lines on the road. And dustbins. And their own farts (I kid you not).

And I love them.

Horse and Pony Breeds

As with dogs, there are many breeds of horse and pony. Some are specifically bred for a particular "job" – for example, all racehorses are thoroughbreds – but many equines, no matter the breed, are "all-rounders", capable of doing a bit of everything, from hacking to dressage to jumping, albeit some more reluctantly than others, and some with greater skill than others.

In the UK we are fortunate to have many breeds of native pony, including the tiny little Shetland pony (originating from the Shetland Isles, so probably so short otherwise they'd get blown over), and the well-known New Forest pony (no prizes for guessing where that originated), and the various Welsh pony breeds (noted for their all-round usefulness, and all-round roundness and deeply rooted obsession with all things edible).

Whilst not a specific breed as such, the term "cob" usually describes a middleweight, mid-height, excessively hairy-legged terrific little all-rounder horse, though they can vary from a "cob-let" (pony-size) to a full-blown carthorse. Rarely appreciated as a "proper" dressage horse, the cob is the decathlete of the horse world in that he will turn his hoof to most things pretty safely and successfully, but he is unlikely to be a world-beater in any specific area. It is a mystery why so many riders who would thoroughly enjoy a cob end up with some deranged, fragile part-thoroughbred to shatter their nerves on, but I suspect there is some element of snobbery involved, as cobs are also often the chosen steed of travellers. But as travelling folk, in my experience, aren't usually stupid, there's probably a reason why they choose cobs, which others could do well to explore…

And while we're on the subject of snobbery, "coloured" horses may be avoided by some for the same association with travellers. "Coloured" in the horse world has a very different meaning to anywhere else – coloured horses are pretty much anything other than brown or black (or grey)! They include palomino (Barbie doll golden horse with white mane and tail), piebald (patches of black and white), skewbald (patches of brown and white) and dun (kind of a brindle thing going on). Coloured horses are pretty marmite – some horsey folk can be snobby about them, while others won't have anything but. For me, in the horse world, as in the real world, I am an All Lives Matter kind of person – I have had my best eventing fun on a piebald cob, I've never met a bad dun, I've been carried round my biggest cross-country courses by a brown horse and now own a chestnut (ginger) and a grey, so I think I can consider myself pretty multi-horsi-cultural.

If someone describes a horse as being "green", it's not their colour they are referring to – horses don't come in green – it is their level of experience. A green horse is an inexperienced, usually young horse. I'm not sure why they are referred to as green; perhaps it reflects the colour their riders' faces turn as their ride resembles more of a roller-coaster than a gentle stroll.

Often bred specifically for dressage and jumping are "warmbloods", of which there are numerous breeds, including the Hanoverian and the Trakehner. Although now also bred in the UK, these breeds originated on the continent, and many UK owners continue to import their competition horses, not least for the opportunity to enjoy a horse-shopping holiday abroad (thereby often allowing the additional benefit of enabling the true cost of their latest purchase to be obscured from their spouse) and for the perceived kudos attached to obtaining an import.

Iberian horse breeds, such as the Andalusian and Lipizzaner, are more unusual. The Andalusian, or PRE, is a centuries-old Pure Spanish Horse breed now generally found in the dressage arena but was noted in history as a war horse. I stumbled into owning one a couple of years ago and he'd be pretty rubbish as a war horse, not that he isn't brave and quick – he's both of those – but because his overwhelming characteristic is that of being absolutely hilarious: his legs fly about, he stamps his foot like an impatient toddler and he wears the most comical expressions. Perhaps as a war horse he could reduce the enemy to a giggling jelly with his antics the same way he does me and we'd win a war that way – sounds better than charging them down being all scary and lairy anyway.

In short, there are many breeds, and almost unlimited cross-breed possibilities, of horses and ponies, each with their own characteristics, strengths and quirks.

And I love them all.

(Apart from some of the thoroughbreds – the ones that are high-maintenance and bonkers, you can keep them.)

Dressage

This complex and demanding sport is categorically *not* a bunch of rich ladies-wot-lunch-but-wot-have-lost-their-nerve-jumping prancing around on their over-priced imported steeds, who are themselves trained to the nth degree by someone who can actually really ride and only allowing said ladies to take to the saddle when the bell goes to start the test.

That would never happen.

I accept that for those without an appreciation for the intricacies involved (and to be fair, often even for those with it) watching a dressage competition can look like pretty much the same horse, with maybe a variation in colour between either bay (brown) or grey (no horse is called "white", no matter how much you think it looks white, even if it's white enough to appear as the "after wash" item in a Persil advert, it's not white, it's "grey") flumping randomly about a white-boarded arena, often to the soundtrack of some dreadful instrumental version of your favourite song, ruining it for you in the process.

However, *real* dressage starts at grassroots and is variously enjoyed by/strikes genuine fear into the hearts of riders of all ages and stages on all manner of horses and ponies – and even a donkey recently! To enter a competition, each rider has to memorise a pre-set routine lasting six or seven minutes of walk, trot and canter movements, such as circles (often barely recognisable as such, usually egg-shaped depending on where the scary photographer is standing or where the exit to go back to the lorry/café is, in turn depending on whether it's the horse or rider whose priorities are drifting along with their accuracy). This is The Test and it will be ridden in front of an eagle-eyed judge, who fills out a results sheet for each competitor, giving them a mark out of 10 for each movement in the test, and often a "helpful" comment too, plus a few more marks for overall impression. The winner is simply the rider with the highest marks. It's a bit like *Strictly* but with hairier legs (I'm not commenting on whether I mean the horses or riders, as with most horsey ladies I know, it's probably both) and less glitter (usually).

The judge is unpaid and frankly on a hiding to nothing given that in every competition only one rider can win and so only one rider will, as a result, like said judge and give their comments the respect and consideration they deserve. The rest of the class will disagree with their scores, treat the judge's comments – if they can read the often dubious handwriting – with scorn, disbelief, anger and despair, will question the judge's eyesight or whether this is really *their* test sheet – surely it must be someone else's? – will spread rumours that the judge is chummy with her class winner, etc., etc. Football referees have it easy compared with the flack dressage judges get, believe me; the only difference is that at least footballers and fans have the good grace to say/shout/sing it to their faces.

There are numerous levels of dressage tests, starting from Intro, then Preliminary, then Novice, then Elementary – all of which sound like they must be tests for those just learning to ride. This is not the case, despite what some judges might think after judging a particularly startling class where their mastery of crafting carefully constructive comments to encourage their eager, but nonetheless quite awful, competitors has been sorely tested. The vast majority of dressage competitors never make it beyond Novice, despite being supremely experienced and perfectly able riders; it's just that the higher levels genuinely are harder, and not merely for those just off the lead rein at a riding school as the names seem to suggest.

Dressage is therefore not for the egotistical. The penultimate level of test, the level one short of Olympic-level, is called "Intermediate" – suggesting that the horses and riders are merely "OK, I suppose", as opposed to reflecting the years and years of training and dedication required to scale such dizzy heights.

Even the official descriptions that go with the marks out of 10 are hardly ego-stroking. For example, a score of 7 out of 10 is really pretty great, most riders would be chuffed to bits to get a score sheet full of 7s. The official description of a 7? "Fairly good" – hardly gushing praise!

I suggest a revision to the official descriptions to something a little more positive, as follows:

Score	Current Official Description	Revised Description
0	Not Performed	Crikey! You have my sympathy
1	Very bad	Still crikey, but a point for not bursting into tears
2	Bad	Maybe the horse would prefer to jump?
3	Fairly bad	Maybe the rider would prefer to knit?
4	Insufficient	Could be worse (see above)
5	Sufficient	There's light at the end of the tunnel, keep going
6	Satisfactory	You've cracked it, good work
7	Fairly good	Awesome, this test sheet's going on Facebook/Instagram
8	Good	Wow, just wow
9	Very good	Jaw-dropping, there are tears in the judge's eyes
10	Excellent	OMG, actual perfection, there are tears in everyone's eyes

In summary, dressage is generally boring to watch, hard to do and not very rewarding.

And I love it.

Show Jumping

Those of you of a certain age may remember watching this on telly when Harvey Smith and David Broom were household names, and the Whitaker boys (the patriarchs of show jumping's most ridiculously talented and successful family) were still bombing about on ponies.

It usually involves one relatively sedate round of jumping over knock-downable poles, followed by (if you don't knock down any such poles) a second round going as fast as you dare without the horse hitting the fences or the rider hitting the floor.

As with dressage, what you might catch on some obscure red-button channel on TV for a few hours a year these days, does not reflect the level of show jumping most of us riders are far more familiar with. The grassroots level of the sport is much more entertaining. The jumps may be considerably smaller, but the equal diminution in control, ability, training and talent (and I absolutely include myself in this description) make for a much more fun sport. The camaraderie amongst competitors usually exponentially increases as the fences decrease in size too.

It's a bit like F1: do you want to watch the formidably talented Lewis Hamilton lead a race from pole position, perform a technically brilliant drive, supported by excellent strategy, to sweep majestically to the top of yet another podium without having to pass another car – or do you want to watch a bit of banger racing?

My level of show jumping is definitely in the banger racing category. I used to be OK at it, on the right horse, but I've never been technically great and since losing my confidence on some dodgy horses, I'm technically, and actually, terrible. A bit like in aviation, where they say that any landing you walk away from is a good one, these days I'm happy just to get from one side of a jump to the other complete with the horse, and that's without divulging how tiny the jump is.

So I keep telling myself, I am also put off from doing show-jumping competitions these days because they can be rather long, drawn-out affairs. Unlike dressage, where several days in advance a competitor is given a *very* specific test start time (tests are usually precisely eight minutes apart!), which appeals to my inner spreadsheet, jumping is far more random. Often one enters on the day, so no one will know whether each class will have six entries or sixty. So then no one knows if your chosen classes, say the fifth and sixth of the day, will start at 10am or 6pm. You might jump your first round, go clear and then have to wait two hours to do the jump off against the clock, just to have your horse lazily clump out a pole. All in all, it's a bit too much hanging around and not enough precision for me.

And that's what I keep telling myself.

Eventing

Usually One-Day Eventing, to be precise, whereby each horse and rider performs a dressage test and a round of show jumps and a round over cross-country jumps all in one frantic, nerve-wracking day. The scores from each phase are amalgamated to find the winner.

Dressage purists would have you believe that the level of dressage found in eventing is, shall we say, substandard, and that may well have been the case once upon a time, when the lowest level of eventing was "Novice" (another misnomer, like the dressage classes, as the jumps at this height were "proper") and you needed a decent jumping horse to survive, let alone win, so a terrible dressage score could easily become academic. However, these days the "starter" classes have far lower jumps, allowing more dressage-oriented horses, and riders, to enter the fray, plus it seems that everyone has generally upped their game across the board.

To go eventing, life is made considerably easier if you have a horse lorry, as opposed to a car and horse trailer, because it is usually muddy and often raining and you'll need somewhere to hide in between each of the phases to avoid hypothermia. A lorry is also somewhere to store your support team and all the changes of saddles, bridles, horse boots and bandages, and changes of clothes needed for each different phase. And a pretty comprehensive first-aid kit and well-stocked bar often come in handy too. Even better is a lorry with its own loo to save all those numerous and increasingly urgent trips to the dreaded and completely disgusting Portaloos before the cross country.

Eventing is really all about the cross country. Usually a minimum of a five-minute gallop, often way more, over fields and up and down hills, jumping solid timber fences, over ditches, hedges and through water. It is set to an optimum time, with penalties for going too slow or even (for the kamikaze amongst us) too quickly. It is fast and potentially dangerous and properly exciting – a good round will have the rider dancing all night, a bad round and the only dancing will be the lights she can see in front of her eyes from the concussion.

Eventing is one of the few sports where not only do men and women compete on level terms (as they do in dressage and show jumping) but where an ordinary one-horse grassroots rider can rub shoulders with and genuinely compete against – and beat – world-class riders, who start their young or inexperienced horses at the lower levels.

Back in the day, I loved it.

Too old and scared now!

Horsey Terms

Hands high (hh) – a horse's height is measured in "hands", despite horses clearly not having any. A "hand" equals four inches because apparently, a standard person's hand is supposed to measure four inches when laid flat on its side. You've just looked at your hand and looked for a ruler, haven't you? Also, because a horse can move his head up and down rather a lot, he isn't measured to the top of his head like us humans; he is measured to a particular point on his back, where it meets his neck, called his withers. A pony can be up to 14.2hh, though your average Shetland pony would be about 10hh, and Shire horses average at about 17hh.

Lunging – no, we riders don't try and mix it up a bit, pick up our swords and try a little fencing, although that would probably be safer. When we "lunge" a horse we attach a long rope to his head and make him go round and round us in a big circle. The idea is to exercise and train the horse with minimum effort from the human. However, the reverse is often true, as the horse trains the human to lead, chase and generally run around far more than the horse would bother doing.

Matchy-matchy – not exclusive to the horsey world but seen by some riders as an absolutely essential element of horse ownership. This is the art of having as much of a horse's tack, equipment and wardrobe to be of identical colour. Items generally regarded as must-haves are matching cloths to go under a saddle, girth (belt to keep the saddle on) or girth cover, leg bandages, fly veils, headcollars and lead ropes. The truly dedicated matchy-matchy fan will also match her own attire to her horse's with identically coloured jodhpurs, sweatshirt, jacket, gloves and riding hat cover. The matchy-matchy fan who needs her spending (and possibly life choices) more closely monitored will have the complete match-matchy set, horse and human, in numerous colours.

Backing a horse – this is neither reversing a horse nor betting on it; it is the process by which a horse is trained to accept a rider. This is also referred to as "breaking" a horse, though it is the usually the poor crash test dummy rider who is far more likely to get broken in the process as the reluctant or frightened horse throws them off by bucking (suddenly doing a handstand, throwing the rider over its head) or rearing (standing on their hind legs, throwing the rider over its bottom) or broncing (all four legs come off the ground at once, horse's nose goes to the floor, with a few back twists thrown in for good measure, sending the rider into orbit and the reason people pay good money to watch rodeos).

The school – much as some of us would love our horses to go and sit in a class and learn every day, that generally isn't an option, so instead we use an arena – or school – to train or exercise our horses in. This may be anything from an area of field marked off with poles or cones up to a professionally installed structure including drainage, substructure, membrane and the choice of a variety of artificial surfaces, costing tens of thousands of pounds, or even hundreds of thousands for an indoor school complex. I can but dream of having an indoor school up here in the Highlands, where winter riding can be sporadic!

So that was your Idiot's Guide to Horses (by which I mean it was written by an idiot), which should see you through any unplanned encounters with someone horsey, any random pub quiz equestrian questions and, more importantly, Bond's memoirs...

Contents

The Beginning

L et me introduce myself.

The name's Bond – no, really, it is. She called me Bond.

I'm pretty sure it's because I'm handsome, athletic, brave, clever and irresistible to the laydeeees (modest too), although she – my human – says it's because when we first met she felt an instant bond between us, soppy human that she is, but then she also says that when she bought me she had to cash in her premium bonds (that's more like it, she is an accountant, after all – perhaps as much mercenary as soppy) to begin our very, very expensive journey together. Oh, and she says I was the 007th horse she viewed during her search for a horse at that time, *and* the 007th horse she had ever owned, so it was inevitable that I would be licensed to thrill. Or a licence for the vets to bill, she is heard to mutter at times.

Some vital statistics for those that would like to visualise the gorgeousness that is me: I am a 16.2hh bright chestnut Trakehner gelding, with three white socks (just like my dad) and a dashing white blaze, which she curses regularly as she says it's wonky and only serves to accentuate my predilection for head-tilting my way through our most important dressage tests, which is obviously nothing to do with her heavy right hand skewing my nose sideways. Oh no.

I mentioned my dad – he is worth more than a mention. I am terribly well bred, you know. Pops was a UK Elite stallion called Holme Grove Solomon. He was a bit of a dish and I am the spitting image of him, if I say so myself (apart from the comedy blaze, his was a discrete white trickle down the *centre* of his therefore far more noble face, as I am unnecessarily reminded all too frequently). He was also apparently an absolute gentleman, which I genuinely have strived to emulate, with only the occasional aberration, which I'm sure is immediately forgiven and forgotten, at least once whatever/whoever I broke has mended, anyway. I looked up "Elite" and it means "superior", which I would say, in my humble opinion, describes me perfectly too; like father like son.

I was bred, born and raised at the rather smart Holme Grove Stud in Bedfordshire, where I was able to spend my formative years turned out with my age group, enjoying precious time as, what she calls, a "proper" horse, while I was youthfully ignorant of, and completely without desire for, such luxuries as rugs and stables. Aaahhh, how I smile now at the cleverness of my life choices, as my slightest of shivers sends her scampering off for the next higher tog-rated rug, and another bale of straw for my already knee-deep bed.

But, so she tells me, I was once what she calls "man enough" to live out happily and healthily as part of a herd, as naturally as possible. I have to admit to taking issue with the "man enough" quip in this instance. I am prepared to accept the slight if her human man lives outside day and night unencumbered by his jeans and fleece-lined hoody uniform, with nothing but a few trees for shelter. But while he gets to snuggle up in his centrally heated house, wearing as many layers as he likes, I fully intend to be afforded the same courtesy (minus the central heating – I'm not *spoilt*, obviously).

So, after many blissful years just chillin' with my bros (see, I'm still down with the kids) at the stud, some genius decided it was time I gained useful employment. I had been lightly backed as a youngster and she has seen brief video evidence of a rather wobbly four-year-old me under saddle at a stud open day, so it wasn't too nasty a surprise to be ridden, but sadly the stud didn't have a rider to bring me on, so at the age of six I was sent away to an experienced and respected dressage sales yard. Now being sent away to boarding school *was* a surprise.

It started off well enough.

I was stabled next to a rather handsome stallion, and also a rather fast railway line, which was a little startling, but, as I generally do, I quickly got used to it.

Side note – that's the way I roll – I don't tolerate change very well (she would say "at all") and *nothing* gets past me: a pole in the school in a different position to my last schooling session – scary; the yard hose reel left slightly unfurled this time – I'll spot it; a piece of rubbish on the floor that wasn't there before – that's not right; the trailer parked in a different spot – something's up… Do you see where I'm coming from? *But*, my two saving graces, so I'm told (hang on, only two?), are: one, any change/difference is perfectly acceptable on the second day/sighting (don't ask me why – I don't make the rules; I just apply them), and two, that what I see when I go out competing doesn't count; the spook-o-meter is reset for each venue, so my first visit is absolutely fine. But all bets are off if the venue makes any changes between my visits…

Anyway, I took to the restriction to a stable, with just short bouts out in a paddock, well enough to begin with, and so my education started.

So she tells me, an advert was published at that point with a suitably large price tag for a deserving-enough person (either with very deep pockets or in happy possession of a rich but resigned-to-their-fate-as-bankroller daddy/mummy/husband/wife) to buy me. She saw this advert and, while obviously admiring my photo and description, had to dismiss it as I was totally out of her price range. Something she would do well to remember now, punching above her weight and all that.

Unfortunately, as time went by, I let the situation get to me and, while still being an absolute gentleman in the stable, really couldn't help myself from expressing, when ridden, my frustration at my newly restricted lifestyle. I was quite supple back then and really threw some shapes, mostly a variety on the handstand. I think I rather fancied myself as quite the break-dancer.

My education shrieked to a halt and my price halved. Enter stage left my can't-resist-a-bargain owner-to-be, whose eagle eyes had spotted my now still not-quite-bargain-basement advert, but who realised I was now within reach of those ill-fated premium bonds.

Apparently when she spoke to the sales yard manager before coming to meet me, he explained *exactly* what I had been up to, making sure she was under no illusion that she was going to see some placid dobbin (hahaha, if he could see me now!), but she was braver/more stupid/desperate back then, so along she came.

I rather think it helped that she had been looking for a horse for months, had travelled around the country to try several, with varying results, from rejecting a little young piebald late-cut chap who despite his green-ness behaved impeccably when she schooled him in a field he'd never been in and even popped a few jumps (too "just nice" apparently, not "look at me" enough – there really is no pleasing some folk) to a bigger stamp of a fellow who she says looked like he was being ridden incredibly carefully and tactfully when demonstrated to her, so when she mounted she wasn't at all surprised to feel his back go rigid, and the moment she put the smallest amount of leg on to ask for walk, he started to rear, at which point she hopped off and said, "No, thank you, not for me" – without so much as taking a stride in walk on the horse!

So, on the back of that, I didn't really have to try too hard to win her over. When she arrived, I was my usual handsome and snuggly self in the stable, which nearly had her handing over a deposit there and then. I decided she looked like she might shape up OK as my human, with a bit of moulding, so aimed to seal the deal by behaving boringly sensibly when demonstrated by the yard manager and ridden by her, much to everyone's surprise.

Despite the fact I hadn't mastered the right canter lead by then, due to my halted education, and my straight lines resembling those of a drunk walking home from a particularly good party, she could see my potential and loved me from that day on, nine years ago now. She was also uber impressed when the high-speed train shot past the arena and I barely flickered an ear at it. Maybe she thought I was a horse that didn't react to things. Bless her.

Even the sales yard manager didn't kibosh the whole thing by being frankly unnecessarily honest once again about my usual antics, in his keenness for her to understand I really wasn't normally the safe and sane chap she had witnessed. He was probably rather regretting dropping my price tag so dramatically. But it was too late, she had fallen under my spell, cue sinister chortling.

My next challenge was the vetting. I had reverted back to my usual self by then and demonstrated for the vet my movement and suppleness, first at the end of a lunge line (the vet reported back to her that no one seemed keen to ride me straight from the stable) and then ridden too under the hapless and reluctant yard jockey after I'd worn myself out a bit. Happily the vet could judge that, in between bucking, plunging and demonstrating all my cool dance moves, I was also demonstrating soundness, and along with his resounding affirmation of my good nature ("No one was actually killed," I believe his words were), it was considered a Passed Vetting. Go me!

A few days later she pitched up to collect me. I must admit I was a little put out at my mode of transport: a trailer... a *trailer*... and not even one of those posh ones with a teeny tiny human house in its nose, just your ordinary Ifor Williams 510 (it doesn't even have air-conditioning!). Oh, the shame – didn't she know who I *was*? I had been hoping for a smart little lorry and I'm sure she could afford one with only a modest extension to her mortgage. She'd buy one if she *really* loved me. But little did I know how I would grow to blooming love my travels in that trailer, and quite where it would take me, but more of that later...

Anyway, a couple of hours later we arrived at my new home, a bit sweaty and stressed after the journey (yes, both her and me). But to my relief and delight I was not only introduced to my two new friends but also released into a lovely big field with them. Her friends Jean and Ian had allowed her to bring me to their home to live with their two geldings, who, to my utter joy, they kept as naturally as possible. We three were allowed to roam freely around the huge field, through the always-open gate onto the yard, where there were hay feeders, and even, if we wanted, into the stables, whose doors remained pinned open. We were only locked into the stables in the foulest of weather.

What a great way to live! Freedom, shelter, companions, food – this was an absolute turning point for me. Things could have turned out so differently if at that point I had gone to live in a place with restricted turnout. My ridden antics would inevitably have continued, if not worsened, which even I can see wouldn't have made for a happy human. My situation could easily have spiralled downwards, just for the sake of the need for a bit of space and freedom for a young horse to make the adjustment from stud baby to riding horse.

We had a lovely arena for me to learn in, and fabulous hacking in the forests of the Surrey Hills. From the very day of my arrival, the only time I bucked was when she tickled or tapped me with that confounded schooling whip. She soon learnt to carry it in such a way that it didn't tickle my bottom accidentally when we were on small circles! Sadly she couldn't simply ride without the whip because I always knew if she did, and would offer my best impression of an elderly and wise riding school dobbin: shuffling slowly, putting in minimal effort, dead to the leg… All she had to do was pick the whip up again – not even use it – and my alter ego was back: young, eager and willing! And they say horses are stupid! (Well, to be fair, that's mainly what her husband says.)

But the giddy days of turning myself inside out to release my frustration were gone, never to return. You see, I really am a genuinely nice chap (rather unkindly she says I'm inclined to be a little lazy too, and all that bouncing about was frankly quite an effort – and that after I saved her a fortune by behaving in such a way as to get my price slashed so she could afford me; that's gratitude for you).

So, as an aside, maybe I should tell you a little about her. Only a little, mind, as this is all about me. It's always all about me, she says. The husband says that too, but he doesn't have quite the same dreamy tone to his voice and soppy look in his eyes when he says it.

Horses 001 to 006

When we met, she had twenty-five-odd years of horse ownership and riding experience as an adult under her belt.

So what I'm saying is, she was no spring chicken.

It also meant she was an OK rider and not completely ignorant about horse management.

As a seventeen-year-old she had bred a foal from a borrowed Welsh mare, who she had put to the National Arab Champion stallion for that year. The result was a 14.1hh bay mare pocket rocket called Soli (001), whom she still owned when my human met me, and who was still fit and well in her mid-twenties at that time, but who was away on loan to a family whose daughter was to benefit from Soli's own brand of wisdom and experience. This apparently largely consisted of applying speed to every aspect of equestrianism, whether it be hacking or jumping. Even dressage was a challenge to be completed against the clock, even at that age – possibly actually even more so at that age, as she had long ago nailed the technique for oh-so-subtly taking charge of her little jockeys, whether they were children or small adults. Our paths would cross in a few years' time, and she still hadn't slowed down then, knocking on thirty years old.

Thankfully my human had lost her need for speed over the years before we met. I am bred for, built for and have the mind set for dressage – and not Soli's version of dressage either. If I were a *Grand Tour* presenter I would definitely be Captain Slow. She absolutely bought me with the intention to give dressage a proper go, having wheeled round dressage tests, after a fashion, as part of something called "eventing".

She tells me the point of eventing, as far as eventers are concerned, is to get through the dressage with gritted teeth and a fake smile at the end, no matter how the test went, and tolerate the show jumping without going into meltdown over some unnecessarily booted-out poles, to get to the nirvana of the cross-country round. She explained cross country to me as like going for a speedy hack round some fields while jumping anything in your path.

Sounds horrendous to me.

An unnecessary waste of energy – especially the jumping bit. I've demonstrated my wisdom to her on the issue on the rare occasions she believed it a possibility I might like to partake in, or even enjoy, this "cross country" nonsense. I point out that the clever horse is the one that goes *round* the jumps, not over them, and not wasting energy or taking unnecessary risks. I've even had to stop smartly at a jump several times so she can get a closer look at just how risky my leaving the ground could be. And how simple the route round the jump is, without all that fuss and, frankly, serious health and safety issues. Somebody could get hurt! They say that golf is the art of ruining a nice walk; cross country does the same for a nice hack if you ask me. But nobody does. Ask me.

Don't get me wrong, I find popping a small (and I do mean small) show jump (poles only, you can keep your scary fillers) rather exciting, and I will tolerate it largely because it occurs in my dressage arena – my safe place, if you will. You see, it's on a *surface* and I approve of surfaces, and cross country? Well, it's not on a surface and there is mud and hills and, heaven forbid, splashy bits and, well, it simply isn't dressage, dhhhharling. I really don't think Daddy would approve.

And another thing. Cross country quite rightly involves us horses wearing protective boots.

I don't do boots.

They make my legs feel weird, so I waggle them around even worse than in that video of me as a gangly four-year-old. I don't even like travel boots – when she used to put them on (she finally gave up after years of my remonstrations) I would stand planted, rooted to the spot, because if I moved at all the boots would just… I don't know… just… *be there.* It got to the stage I could just about tolerate moving my front legs in a relatively horse-like fashion in them, with my back legs still planted, which resulted in some interesting yoga-like positions, and when finally forced to move my back legs as the only alternative to performing an undignified belly-flop, I'd kick, waggle and hop my way as clumsily and awkwardly as possible from stable to trailer, where I travelled like a rock. It took years for the penny to drop, but eventually even she acknowledged I was more likely to hurt myself (or someone else) *because* of the boots, pre-travel, than I would travelling sans boots. Finally, no boots. Simples. Bless her, she has taken some training, but with patience and persistence I have managed over the years to make her exactly the human (some say "slave") I wanted.

Gosh, somehow I've gone from telling you a little about her to talking entirely about me again – can't imagine how that happened. I'm not normally self-obsessed at all.

So, yes, in her PB (Pre-Bond, absolutely categorically *not* Personal Best) years, she did eventing, mainly on her legend of a horse, 002, a bay gelding (as is compulsory in eventing, I understand) 16.1hh Irish Draught x Thoroughbred, going by the name of Rubbish. I kid you not. That amazing beast took her round enormous tracks, taught her everything, was a gentleman and a hero, and spent his entire life under the name Rubbish, simply because as a foal the poor fellow had a penchant for foraging through rubbish bins given any opportunity. Oh, the shame of it. Literally named and shamed.

While she still wore brave pants, she also did a little breaking and training (hence why my reported antics didn't faze her) and had a grand time competing at riding club level on all sorts of friends' and clients' horses and ponies (it's OK, she's short) at anything she could – dressage, show jumping or eventing. Not showing, though. She never has been one for tack-cleaning…

Her absolute favourite of these was a 15hh coloured Irish "Sports Horse" (cob) called Harry, who is another legend by all accounts, owned by her good friend Jenny. Whilst maybe not your classic stamp of eventer, the dressage judges adored him if for nothing more than breaking the monotony of bay TBs; he was nimble to show jump and had the heart of a lion cross country. Because of the shortness of his little hairy legs, he was always going to struggle to meet optimum times, but his amazing ability and willingness to jump a fence from crazy angles and with limited approach meant they cut every corner possible to strive for the quickest possible time. Her competitive highlights with him included show jumping for the awesomely friendly (and largely alcoholic) Newlands Corner Riding Club team at the Royal International Horse Show at Hickstead – one round against the clock, which he blitzed and their team won, and being placed in the Three Day Event at the National Riding Club Championships after an awesome XC round, trotting into the ring to collect their prize to a collective "awwwww" from the crowd at the sight of the only slightly overgrown pony competing rather successfully beside leggy TBs, who had two hands on him, as it were.

Talking of TBs, 003 and 004 were both ex-racehorses.

The first of these, 003 was a "project" buy, bought locally and cheaply from the field. Bumble had been out of racing for longer than he had been in it, having been entirely unsuccessful on the track, and was then kept by a lady for occasional hacking but mostly grass-mowing

– lucky devil. My human reschooled him and got him popping a course of jumps and enduring what could loosely be described as a very basic dressage test. He was a typical thoroughbred – sharp, clever, opinionated, but actually a real sweetie too.

Long before she had even thought of advertising him as the finished product, the yard at which she kept him and Rubbish held a little in-house fun show. Bumble had a crack at the dressage and jumping and, in a most un-ex-racehorse-like way, the fancy dress (he was, rather appropriately, deputy to Rubbish's sheriff). I am grateful to my human for never expecting such demeaning behaviour from me – parading around in my winner's sash with rosettes dripping from my bridle is one thing, doing the walk of shame round a show ring wearing a tutu as one of the *Fantasia* elephants is quite another.

He can't have done a bad job because one of the show's spectators, a lady called Victoria, fell in love with Bumble on sight and, despite the fact that she hadn't actually been looking for a horse to buy, and he wasn't actually fully ready for sale, a few days later she returned to the yard to try him.

My human insisted she try him in the arena first, thoroughly against Victoria's protestations, as her passion was for hacking and cross country. She hated schooling and, after she had endured a few minutes in the arena, to her enormous relief they went out for a hack with her laughing that if she did indeed buy him, that would be the last time he would have to see the inside of a school…

Little did they all know…

She did, of course, buy him. And now, seventeen years later, still owns him, having never once jumped a cross country fence on him but having got him up to competing at medium-level dressage through hard work, resilience and sorely tested patience. He now resides in quite the Surrey dressage horse spa and must be one of the luckiest horses alive, to have found an owner who has adored him through all manner of tantrums, endless spooking, falls, broken bones, losses of confidence, lameness and health issues. And I know all this because, again, despite everything that horse threw at her, she and my human became and remain best of friends.

She still likes to ask for her money back every now and then, though.

The other ex-racehorse, 004, was a very sweet TB my human got straight from Walter Swinburn's flat racing yard, a secretary at her work having been in the syndicate that owned him. She had hoped he would be her next eventer but turns out he had even less natural jumping ability than I, which is saying something, and after too many speedy, wobbly, awkward launches at fences he was probably largely responsible for her hanging up her brave pants (horrible image, sorry). He quite took her confidence at jumping away, for which I will be eternally grateful to him, and despite him competing at affiliated dressage, her trainer described attempting to progress him up the levels as trying to fit a square peg in a round hole (a brutal honesty my human was actually very grateful for, to save both her and the horse from an eternally uphill and ultimately unsatisfying struggle) and he was sold after four years, as a well-schooled hack to a lady in her seventies who had always had TBs and "wasn't ready to retire to a cob yet" and who found him delightful.

There was another winter project buy: 005. This time a pretty little grey mare, 15hh Connemara x Thoroughbred type, called Willow. She took to both dressage and jumping with natural flair and my human thought she would make a teenager very happy indeed. However, in the spring, when she advertised her, a fairly local posh hacking centre was interested in her as a lead horse for the staff to ride. My human had such confidence in the mare that she agreed to their required terms of having a week's trial and so was horrified when she received a call some days later to hear that the horse was to be returned as she had started headshaking and had threatened to rear several times. My human's inclination was to simply not believe them and that they, for whatever reason, didn't want her but felt they had to make up some excuse.

But on bringing her home she found their story to be true. My human was mortified, as the horse had shown no such inclination previously, and was also concerned in case she had somehow been injured during her time away. A check over revealed no obvious physical issue, but my human isn't one for giving up on a horse that easily. A little time and investigation later, she established that simply riding the horse in a nose net (mesh attached to her bridle to cover her nose, filtering insects and pollen) prevented any issues. And so she was sold, with full disclosure, to a lovely lady, to be used as an all-rounder.

Finally, 006, my human stumbled into owning entirely unintentionally. A friend of the lovely Jean and Ian owned a horse that she was no longer able to ride, through no fault of his own. She couldn't bear to even go and see him as it just broke her heart not being able to fulfil the dream of enjoying her little horse anymore. He was costing her a fortune at his Surrey horse hotel, as she was paying not only for the all-inclusive package but also for someone to exercise him regularly, and so she just wanted someone she could trust to rehome him. Jean suggested my human and so, a few emails and not many days later, my human headed off to collect little Teddy.

Sadly, the Teddy she collected was not the glossy, handsome fit picture of health she had seen a couple of photos of. He was underweight and had muscle wastage from lack of work; his thick unclipped coat, while appropriate for his name, merely hid a lack of care by the hotel. My human was disgusted at their treatment both of him and of his loving owner who had no idea her beloved horse was in such a condition.

Teddy was whisked away, wormed and gradually brought back to health and strength. And then what a lovely little fellow he was! An eye-catchingly attractive 15.2hh dun Connemara cross, he was a smart little prelim/novice dressage horse, who was also perfectly capable jumping and so easy to do in all ways. To sum up how safe and kind this little chap was, Jean had told my human of a day when his previous owner had hacked Teddy out alone, over a motorway bridge, cantered quietly across an open heath and, upon returning to the horse hotel and dismounting, realised that for the whole ride his snaffle bit had been wedged *under* his mouth and not in it!

Teddy was not a difficult horse to find a lovely home for!

And that is *quite* enough about other horses and her; let's get back to the all-important *me*. Oh, I suppose I should add that by trade she's an accountant, whatever that is – sounds like an excuse to sit in front of a computer screen or two pretending to work when actually she's watching YouTube videos of how to train one's horse to carry his own blinking head for once. Whatever she does, as long as it keeps me in the manner to which I have become accustomed, then I will let it continue.

That really is enough about her for now.

A Happy Start

So there I was at Jean's, living, learning and loving life. Many a glorious hack was enjoyed, particularly the pub rides which meant we horses could graze while our humans sipped at some vile-looking discoloured water which made them all relaxed and daft on the ride home.

It was near the start of one such hack that witnessed the one and only time (so far) that she has fallen off me.

If you can call it falling off.

Is it possible to fall off at the halt?

Apparently so.

It wasn't even after any discoloured water; it was before.

And it wasn't my fault. Categorically not.

Maybe.

I shall explain. On arrival at the car park entrance to the forest, she spotted a lost dog. Luckily Jean knew where it had come from so my human hopped off me, gave my reins to Jean and ran the dog back to its home while we waited in the car park. On her return she led me to stand beside a bank (the mound-of-earth type, not the cash-dispensing type) to assist her stumpy little legs to get back on me. The horse-bank-human distancing and placement was all a bit awkward and not quite right, and I "might have" helpfully stepped sideways *towards* her at just the point of no return as she launched herself off the bank at me. Result – she shot headfirst straight across my back instead of onto it, completed a full somersault and landed on her feet (ish) on the other side of me.

Jean, to her credit, didn't laugh as much as one might have expected, but that may have been in case my human reminded her of the time she also "mis-fired" onto her, at best, nervous-to-mount steed Winston, whereby, as they were all mounting up to start their ride, Jean managed to land perfectly on Winston's back.

Behind the saddle.

The already-nervous Winston froze, as did Jean, who just oh-so-slowly turned her head to my human and said quietly, "What do I do now, Ali?" Thereafter was an exquisite scene of beautiful slow motion where no one wanted to be the one to startle Winston into broncing Jean into the next county, instead repeating slow and over-enthusiastic "*good boy*"s over and over and over, as if pure repetition alone would convince him into making it so, while my human moved so slowly to his head to hold him and reassure him while Jean would somehow quietly shuffle over the cantle and into the generally accepted standard riding position *on* the saddle. It only worked! But by then I think everyone's legs had turned to jelly and the ride was abandoned in favour of a calming cup of tea. Or something.

Meanwhile, mounting gymnastics aside, my schooling education was back on track and, truth be told, I rather enjoyed it. I liked nothing more (and still do when the mood takes me) than pinging along in my big flashy trot, happily ignoring the increasingly less subtle attempts from The Short One to try to regain some balance and introduce maybe something else to my one-trick pony repertoire.

Inevitably the time came when my competitive dressage career would be launched. I was certainly concerned when the trailer was hauled out – surely I wasn't moving home again? That had been the only reason for travel so far in my life. I'll admit I was worried and resisted loading (not quite as well as a cat trying to avoid being manhandled into a travel basket by bracing all four paws against the sides, but if my hooves had allowed it I'd have given it a shot at the trailer entrance), but that blinking little human can be a stubborn loader and I gave in after not many minutes. Note to self: must stick to my guns next time. Anyway, I made her feel guilty as hell by shaking from head to foot once loaded (literally shaken, not stirred), but did that stop her driving me away? Did it heck. She'd be blowed if her annual tack-cleaning was going to go to waste.

Anyway, long story short, at the competition I behaved as expected in a completely new environment suddenly surrounded by strange horses coming and going and working around me – I alternated between spooking, tension and total lack of confidence about going forward. Apparently, our test scores were not world-beating! But, as the vet said of my vetting, "No one was killed," and we weren't last – even mid-table in the second test – so in many respects I think it was a win.

She took it on the chin and, armed with the knowledge of how I might respond to a competition environment, went back to my education for a few more months before our second outing. We went through the not loading – loaded (doh, smacks forehead) – shaking routine before heading off. Same venue – for reassurance, apparently (mine or hers?) – and, I'm not sure quite how it happened but we won both classes with over seventy per cent. And that was the first time (of many, I might add, not a little smugly) that she cried happy tears on seeing our competition results. That day rather sealed my fate too, to share many a dressage adventure (yes, they are a real thing) with her, along with our other adventures.

An outing or two later, the judge of one class caught up with my human by the scoreboard and, having realised she was standing beside her winner, very amusingly took my human rather conspiratorially to one side and said that she was so glad it turned out we had won as the horse we had beaten into second place was currently for sale for a truly astronomical price – six figures, apparently – and while she acknowledged it had world-class breeding, she didn't like the way its training was going and so just couldn't mark it higher. My human was over the moon at the high praise for her own training, though I'm not sure I quite liked the way she looked at me whilst thinking about what she could do with a six-figure sum… Even without her calculator she knew that would be turning quite the profit on my purchase and theoretical sale. Happily (for me), a theory was all it remained.

Alas, as is the way in the world, this bubble of blissful life and positivity inevitably had to burst.

Whilst us three geldings generally got on well at Jean's, unfortunately trouble was brewing between Samson and me. Samson is a young Irish chap, a big, solid, easy, willing type who unfortunately didn't appreciate some fancy-pants Trakehner getting in his face all the time. It's not my fault; I'm just a very friendly chap, although my human says I have no concept of personal space for either humans or other horses. To be fair, she's probably right.

So, you may have guessed what's coming, Samson and I came to blows a few times. I got a nasty slice out of my chest once, and he got a hock injury another time. Finally, the humans decided enough was enough and separated us, which was tricky given the previous openness of our field/yard/stable space. A new fence was erected and I can tell you, I was Not Impressed. Samson and his chum one side, and me the other. No, no, no. They could just wander away from me at will! I do *not* do alone. And thus started my life-long habit of fence-pacing to demonstrate my angst. Many a time since this has got me (and her) in trouble with yard owners. Up and down I'd go, quickly wearing a path, destroying the grazing anywhere near the fence and gate. I became a one-horse mud-making machine.

At Jean's I'd done so much damage, and had been so stressed, that Jean suggested removing the fence and trying us all out together again. My human spent many a sleepless night mulling it over and finally, tearfully, said to Jean she would find somewhere else for me. She said she just couldn't risk me getting injured again and, while I appreciate her devotion, I have to say I was shocked. I mean, it's not like the vets were called *every* time we came to blows, and each of us wasn't out of work for more than a few months each time when it did get out of hand... Not sure I can see what the fuss was about; I don't mind having time off, and the vets are all lovely people each and every time one of them comes to see me.

But her decision was made, research done – she'd prepared spreadsheets on it and everything. I was off to pastures new. She says in fact I was lucky that *we* were off to pastures new and not just that I was off to go and complicate someone else's life given how long she'd been with Jean and Ian.

Pastures Old

(This is largely not about me,
so I'm not sure why it's even included -
surely it's all about me?)

She first met Jean and Ian when they needed help bringing their horses back into work after a break of over a year due to other commitments. At that time, they didn't have an arena at home as Jean found riding in an enclosed area terrifying and Ian had zero interest in going round and round in circles for some inexplicable reason. I can't understand it myself; I have found nothing more comforting over the years than training in my safe place. My human says it satisfies my OCD tendencies and need for repetition and nicely avoiding change. And she can't pretend she doesn't love it too. The later addition of an arena to Jean's home was entirely, one hundred per cent, no getting away from it, the fault of my human.

Anyway, not to be put off by the lack of her own safe place to re-start the boys, it was arranged to borrow a neighbour's rather smart indoor arena, which wasn't being used. And who doesn't have a spare indoor arena knocking around? This is Surrey, after all. They never actually met the neighbour – apparently a bit of a recluse – they communicated purely by answerphone message, and payment for arena hire was entirely in whisky. All very normal, I assume.

Ian's horse, Kelpi, a home-bred 17.2hh giant of a grey on which my human equivalent of a Shetland pony looked frankly ridiculous, couldn't have been easier to bring back into work, which is lucky as Shorty would have had her work cut out if he'd ever decided to use just a fraction of his strength against her. But he was as gentle and kind as he was huge. He even had a bit of a talent for the schooling thing, much to Ian's total lack of interest, but the image was somewhat spoilt by the fact that he dished so badly it was hard to tell if he was performing working trot or breaststroke.

Jean's boy Winston, he of the mounting nervousness, was a different matter. Happily, the mounting issue was his only issue – if you could get on, likely you'd stay on and have a lovely ride. But many an hour was spent following him round the indoor school with a mounting block, my ever-patient and persistent human calming and soothing until probably sheer boredom broke him down long enough for her to nip aboard.

The only time she failed to get on at all was the only time she thought she'd try a different method and raised her voice to him. He went absolutely garrety, like she'd beaten him around the head with a hot poker, broke away from her, tore through the arena gate and galloped down the lane home, followed by a huffing and puffing red-faced short lady doing her best to keep up.

She didn't try the shouty thing again.

For all Shorty's persistence and experience, it was Jean herself that found the best method for mounting Winston.

Food.

I'm not sure why it hadn't occurred to anyone before; he was a Welshie, after all, and he'd give his right arm for a carrot. Well, more accurately, he'd take *your* right arm off for a carrot. Anyway, turns out all it took was the application of carrot to horse at just the right moment and his rider would be in the saddle before he'd taken his second bite, or, more importantly, remembered to sidestep away from the mounting block in mock fear. They just had to remember to take carrots with them on their pub rides or it was a long walk home.

And so began many happy years of my human hacking round the Surrey hills with Jean or Ian, or both once she'd snuck her own horse(s) there. She learnt many things in this time, including why she would never have made it as a medic, or a carer – or a mother, for that matter. The moment of epiphany was after a gallop, in which the combination of uneven ground and Kelpi's ever wildly flailing legs had tripped him up, sending both he and Ian crashing to the floor. Kelpi jumped up immediately and looked fine. Ian did not.

Winston, my human's steed for the ride, thought the prone body on the floor looked terrifying and refused to approach immediately, for which my human was secretly rather grateful as, truth be told, she too was somewhat terrified at Ian's still form. Thankfully, after what felt like an hour, but which was probably actually only about thirty seconds, and while my human was still valiantly, but not necessarily whole-heartedly, trying to tug a reluctant Winston forwards with as much success as pulling a cross between a bus and a mule, Ian stirred and sat up.

He had got away relatively lightly with a broken toe and concussion. But, oh boy, that concussion. That was when my human realised she was woefully deficient in the required levels of patience and compassion for dealing with poorly people. Poorly horses are another matter entirely. If it had been Kelpi on the floor she would have stayed with him day and night, done whatever was needed, or Kelpi limping home, she would have tried to carry him, giving him all the time and reassurance and kindness he could wish for, but a fellow human? ... Meh... shrugs...

Of course, straight away Ian asked what had happened. My human kindly explained in detail where they had been, that they had been galloping, Kelpi had tripped, how they both fell and that Ian must have hit his head as he was thrown to the ground and knocked out. Once Ian was on his feet and they were walking/limping back to the forest car park for Jean to pick up Ian, following my human's phone call, Ian asked again what had happened and, pointing at Kelpi, asked if had he been riding Tilly (Kelpi's by that stage long-dead mother). A bit more worried now, my human explained again, at slightly less length, what had happened. And so this went on… and on… repeated over and over, like in the film *Groundhog Day*: Ian asking what happened, my human's responses getting briefer and less patient, till she had perfected the response to something like, "Yes, you fell off Tilly."

Happily, no permanent damage was done – to Ian or to their friendship – but my human recognised that, in so many ways, she had chosen the correct career path and, indeed, life path.

Another "emergency" at Jean and Ian's involved my human's ex-racehorse Masterman, known to all as "M" – honestly, she isn't a James Bond addict. She hasn't had horses called Blofeld or Pussy Galore – this was purely coincidence! And her M was in no way whatsoever a wise, sensible, respected leader like James Bond's boss, as demonstrated on the fateful day my human got a phone call at work to say that "M was stuck in a tree".

She had no more detail than that at that stage, as it was a third-hand message by the time she was contacted, so she jumped in her car and tore towards Jean's with images filling her head of a fire engine extending its ladder to reach a trembling and, frankly, particularly stupid horse clinging to the higher branches of a tree like some sort of super-sized cat rescue. A further thought running through her head was, "No more TBs, I'm getting me a nice, sensible cob."

Because this wasn't M's first field incident. A couple of years earlier he had come in from a nice day out in a field completely devoid of sharp objects – or any objects, for that matter – looking like he'd gone several rounds with Tyson Fury. And lost. Specifically, he had the most enormous swelling, the size of a tennis ball, over one eye, completely closing it. Now my human isn't normally quick to call the vets in for every cut and scrape (too tight, I say; she says it's called experience), but even she could see that maybe some anti-inflammatories might be in order.

Turns out he'd managed to fracture his skull. Lord knows how. Even the vet was extremely concerned, firstly that he would lose the eye, as the size of the swelling was crushing all the squishy bits (tell me if I'm getting too technical for you). Such was the concern that the vet came out twice a day for a week, even saying she would only charge for a fraction of the visits as she was fascinated by his case as she'd never seen such an injury from which a horse actually survived... "How lovely," thought my human, "something to think about in the wee small hours..." But, as the "stuck in the tree" incident a couple of years later proved, he not only survived his fractured skull but completely recovered with no diminution in his TB intellect...

For a while he had a *Tom and Jerry* cartoon-style bump the size of an egg sticking out of his forehead, but all that meant was she didn't plait his forelock when they went out competing in case she was eliminated for riding a unicorn. Do the rules specifically exclude unicorns? I think not!

Inevitably, the truth of the "stuck in a tree" incident didn't involve a single fire engine or ladder, and was a little more mundane, but still particularly stupid, in my humble opinion, because M had rolled beside a tree and somehow got a leg caught in the "V" made by two tree trunks. Once extracted, apart from a few cuts and scrapes, nothing was damaged other than his pride. Oh, and the tree. M's delicate little TB legs didn't so much as make a dent in it, but the lovely souls Jean and Ian didn't want to risk any further horse-eating tree incidents and immediately cut it down.

So, these were just a few examples over the years that demonstrate the length and depth of friendship and horsey camaraderie that my human was walking away from by choosing to put my safety first. Did I feel sad for her and desperately guilty? Well, as she said above about her compassion for fellow humans during Ian's concussion... Meh... shrug... More importantly, what were these pastures new for me?

Pastures New

The much-researched and spreadsheeted challenge to find my perfect residence brought me to a livery yard in Reigate.

Yes, I had upgraded from the equine equivalent of kipping on a mate's sofa to a proper horse hotel, complete with staff! My human's conveniently unaudited calculations had resulted in her conclusion that it was cheaper to pay some other lucky beggar to shovel my golden nuggets and cater to my every need, while she instead used the time at her desk, in theory to earn more than such service was costing her. Win-win, she called it. Part livery, they call it. Lazy dereliction of her duties, I call it. Virtually abandonment, the RSPCA calls it.

Obviously, she had chosen this particular hotel by putting my needs first, but coincidentally it was five minutes from her office, was a child-free yard (she doesn't actively *hate* children – she's actually met one or two that she quite liked – but apparently a definite appeal was avoiding a yard full of bitchy, gossiping, judgemental, glamorous, skinny, confident teenage girls – mainly because she was too old and chunky to join them) and the yard was full of smart Surrey horses owned by ladies that lunch rather than shovel, which was a set she rather fancied being a part of. So impressed was she, she even cleaned my tack before we arrived!

She had met the yard owner/manager (YOM) prior to arrival and judged her sufficiently experienced and capable to be entrusted with my care. She also rather liked her at their first meeting and so was, to say the least, a little perturbed when the moment we arrived – literally, she hadn't even unloaded me from my, by now, trusty trailer – a long-standing livery there greeted her with, "Watch out for YOM, she likes things just so, but don't take it personally when she shouts at you – it's just her way."

So in one swift move it seemed that she had removed me from my bully to find herself a bully of her own. Nice work. Bet *that* wasn't on her spreadsheet.

Turns out YOM wasn't that bad. Mostly. To be fair, she'd probably had more than a reasonable share of idiot humans to deal with over the years and had perfected her way of keeping everyone safe and well, if not entirely happy, and her stables and fields and their inhabitants intact. As long as my human didn't question any change and kept her head down, she was fine, and the ladies-wot-lunch, and those-wot-had-to-earn-a-living-to-keep-us-fine-beasts-in-hotels-and-vets, were all lovely too. She didn't have to clean my tack nearly as much as she had feared.

The hacking there was either around well-to-do Reigate Heath, where matchy-matchy abounded, complete with golf course (imaginatively named Reigate Heath Golf Club) and professional dog-walkers at every turn, or up the extraordinarily steep Reigate Hill, over the motorway bridge (she stuck my nose between my knees so I couldn't see the scary hell that is the M25 whizzing below my hooves – knew all that long and low work in the school would come in handy one day and, frankly, I was too knackered after the climb up the hill to resist) and on to the blissful spaces of Walton Heath.

Alongside Walton Heath runs another golf course – you guessed it, Walton Heath Golf Club. Why aren't they more imaginative with golf club names? Why is there no Whack Your Balls Here Club, Free Your Balls Club, Balls Up Club? Perhaps it's the gelding coming out in me, but I don't understand it.

Anyway, balls to the side, these clubs are pretty protective over their greens and, aware that their course was open to the heath, and that said heath was much-frequented by dolloping great half-tonne horses and their iron-clad feet, rumour had it that there was a £50 fine for each and every hoof-print indent in their immaculate greens. Not one hundred per cent sure how this was to be policed – whether alleged offenders were to be chased down by furious men wielding clubs or equally furious but possibly fatter men in golf buggies, I don't know, but what I *do* know is that if either such horror tried to chase me down I'd find a turn of speed that would have Frankie Dettori leaping from my back in no time, and they'd never catch me.

In theory.

Turns out, in reality, I managed a pretty impressive medium canter on the occasion that she and I were chased from the heath onto the golf course by an out-of-control dog. My human was horrified, I like to think at my astonishing turn of speed, but more likely because she didn't have her calculator on her to tot up the potential cost of all those hoof-prints. However, no furious men in alarming jumpers appeared and don't tell anyone, but I think we got away with it.

Dressage Highs Part One

Meanwhile, back in the safety of the arena, my dressage education was progressing. We had qualified for the Pet Plan Area Festivals at Prelim and Novice and the long-awaited/prepared for/feared weekend of the festival arrived. Happily, it was at my favourite venue, Pachesham Equestrian Centre, and so for the Prelim on Saturday I gave her a happy-favourite-venue kind of test, which she seemed pleased with. We were the last to go in the test, in a pretty large class, and when we got back to our trailer she made a huge fuss of me and started to untack when Linda – Mrs Pachesham, if you will – approached her and said, "I don't know why you're untacking, you're needed for the prize-giving," followed by, "You *won*!" Qualified for the national championships!

To my embarrassment she burst into tears and gave me the biggest hug, whilst making some strange squeaking noise, like a mouse on a roller-coaster. To say she was chuffed to shreds would be quite an understatement and that the stresses of the yard move and so much else coming flooding out was both amusing and alarming to witness. Thankfully she pulled herself together; we attended the prize-giving and I got my sash, which was really all that mattered. I must say, I do look dashing in a sash, and it was a lovely vivid blue which totally complemented my fine chestnut coat. The photographer was all over me, there was applause and I was much complimented. I approved, I really did. Until some fool mentioned that some other winners had completed their lap of honour with a leap over an arena hedge. Seriously? Do I look like some Irish bog hunter? I think not. And I might scratch my sash on the hedge. No. No, no, no.

Bless my human – she was on such a high that she didn't want to ruin it. She seriously considered not returning the next day for the Novice Area Festival. We'd only done a handful of tests at that level so she knew we wouldn't be competitive. I'd done so well on the Saturday, so was it selfish to ask me to go back out on the Sunday, etc., etc.

Thankfully she decided to go, because I do like a party; it does lift me and I really don't find the travelling or whole event tiring. Funnily enough, we were also last to go in the Novice. When we arrived, the human's good friend Jenny and her super-cob Harry were there, and Jenny was hugely excited as they were currently sitting in second place, and the top two qualify for the nationals, so she was keeping a close eye on scores as they went up.

I repeated the pleasant style of test I had performed the previous day and, to my human's genuine astonishment, and then abject horror when she realised what we'd done, we came second, qualifying for the nationals at Novice as well as at Prelim and, yes, bumping poor Harry out of the qualifying places. To Jenny's credit, she didn't punch my human on the nose or slash her tyres or, worst of all, post a photo of her with really appalling hat hair on Facebook; instead she rolled her eyes, no doubt swore a bit and they hugged and remained friends. Because that's what friends do.

Even better, later Jen got a wildcard and came to the nationals the following year too!

Soli

I previously mentioned my human's slightly bonkers but undeniably amazing home-bred pony. Well, not long after I had checked in to my smart Reigate horse hotel, her loan "home for life" wanted to hand her back as the daughter wanted something "more appropriate" to do dressage on. My human couldn't understand it – that pony could get a rider through a dressage test quicker than any steed she'd ever known, so what more could a child want? But she was thrilled to have Soli back after so many years with three really excellent loan families.

So, after a quick reshuffle at the stables, and of my human's creaking finances, Soli came to join me at my Reigate hotel. In order to prevent the creaking finances from actually snapping, Soli and I had to take the socially embarrassing step down from full hotel services to B&B – yep, my human was back to looking after me, picking up after me and had the added joy of doing it all for Soli too, and all before her 8am work start time. She's so lucky to have us.

This would have been fine (in my eyes) if I had been what she regularly refers to as a "normal" horse. And let me say, I'm not sure I appreciate the withering look this comment is often accompanied by. I believe what she is referring to is that I have certain preferences – basically, I prefer that all other horses in the vicinity are doing exactly what I'm doing, and at exactly the same time as me. Maybe it's a control thing, maybe it's a comfort thing, maybe it's an OCD thing. What it *isn't*, oh despairing human, is a deliberate attempt to sabotage the security of my place at that particular hotel by winding up the YOM with my field-pacing (if we horses are not all brought in at the same time) and screaming from my stable (if we horses are not all turned out the same time).

It just looks that way.

The depth of my... ahem... personality... was to some extent disguised when the YOM looked after me, as she brought me in and out at the same time as all the other hotel guests, so it wasn't much of an issue. However, it soon (after the first morning on B&B) was made clear that the only way my existence there would be tolerated by the YOM would be if the turning out/bringing in process was organised with military precision, so in future the B&B-ers were to attend the yard at the YOM's turning out and bringing in times, so all us horses were moved as one herd.

It really was like a daily exercise at boot camp: horrible to be at the wrong end of but blooming funny to watch. There was my human and the other main B&B-er, coincidentally both qualified and respected accountants, both forty-several years old, grumpily but obediently dancing to the tune of the fearful sergeant major to avoid the equine hotel equivalent of being court-martialled. This went on for a surprisingly long time but could never have lasted indefinitely. To be fair to YOM, she didn't flatly ask my human to leave.

Actually, that's not true; at one point she did, but my human somehow managed to grant us a stay of execution.

While all this was going on, the lovely Jean sadly lost Winston and, while she was missing riding, came over and rode Soli (Jean is tiny so didn't trouble the 14.1hh Soli) up to Walton Heath with me and the human (avoiding the expensive golf course). Jean loved Soli's eagerness and sense of fun, and so, long story short, a few days later Soli went to live at Jean's – a very happy outcome for all, including Jean and Ian's grandchildren, who also got to ride her, and reconnecting my human with Jean and Ian, and reconnecting Soli with part of a previous loan family, who regularly rode with them. Soli lived out her years very happily and healthily there, still enjoying her weekly hack, still leading horses a fraction of her age and twice her size, still charging off at a gallop whenever she chose, right up to the day, aged nearly thirty-two, when she lay down in the field and didn't get up.

Dressage Highs Part Two

Our attendance at the Pet Plan National Championships was touch and go for a while. Apparently, there was some highly infectious horse disease going about which made it risky for us horses to meet up socially (sound familiar?). The competition wasn't to be cancelled but there were some that thought it should be, despite assurances from the organisers that there would be bio-security measures in place reminiscent of a foot-and-mouth disease outbreak.

My human spoke to my vet, did a lot of pointless googling whereby she garnered a different opinion from every forum she stumbled across, hummed and hawed, lost sleep, but finally decided it should be safe for us to attend, with the support of the vet and of the YOM, who had to be happy that I wasn't bringing a risk of infection back to our yard. It was proper serious stuff.

The nationals were being held at Hartpury, about a four-hour drive away – my longest-ever journey, which also made my human twitchy, but we left at midday on the Friday to give us ample time to arrive at the competition venue where I would be stabled for the duration of the weekend show, before they closed the vet gates at 7pm. The vets were to meet each one of the hundreds of competing horses on arrival, to check the temperature and general health of each horse in the light of the infectious disease. Any horses failing the inspection would be immediately sent home.

Unfortunately, the road gods were not smiling upon us. Our four-hour journey became five, and then six. My human was frantic: should she turn around and give up; what if we arrived after 7pm; would we get spun round for another marathon journey home? Luckily, she at least had the good sense to phone the venue, who were lovely, reassuring her that we weren't the only ones struggling, that the vets had agreed to stay until 8pm and arrivals after that would simply be quarantined until they could be checked the next day. While that placated her to some extent, that didn't seem to stop her from driving me at warp speed when possible until we arrived, at about two minutes to eight. I think she dropped the ramp of the trailer on arrival, expecting to find me mushed against the rear trailer doors from the G force, or at the very least a wobbly, shaking, sweaty wreck from the length of the journey. Of course, I was absolutely fine, contentedly still chewing on my hay net. I am Bond, after all – shaken not stirred and all that. She was definitely more of a wreck than me – good job they weren't checking *her* temperature, or blood pressure, for that matter.

We had a delightful weekend. I behaved myself impeccably, of course, settled into my stable, wasn't spooky (because I had never seen the arenas before so they didn't qualify on my spook-o-meter as they couldn't have changed if I'd never been in them before – all very logical) and gave her two very pleasant tests. Unfortunately, turns out "pleasant" doesn't quite cut it at this level. We ended up sixteenth in both classes, which out of the UK isn't so bad, I'll take that, but my human came away with a couple of valuable lessons: the first simply that maybe some training wouldn't be a complete waste of time or money, and the second, what turned out to be a life lesson she would shortly act upon, that she could drift along, accepting and ignoring that what she had wasn't right, or she could take some risks, make some changes, go through a period of struggle and maybe, just maybe, it could all be way. way better at the end of it.

Whoa, that was a bit deep.

Time to lighten things up with some vets' bills.

Time Out

Yep, after the honour of competing at the nationals, and a season progressing and competing successfully, I started to feel a bit not right.

My back started to hurt.

Unfortunately, unable to simply say the words, "Oy, missus, my back hurts, call the vet," we had to go through weeks, if not months, of torment. It wasn't so bad early on; it just hurt a bit some days. Some days it might depend what we were doing. I remember vividly one particular jumping session where I went bananas and did three victory laps at the buck after every fence, but she couldn't tell if that was just excitement or horror (she had dared to jump me in a *field*, like a common showjumper!) or pain.

Another time I was particularly "naughty" (as she read it) up on the heath, so she made me go all the way around again until I "behaved". I might have been acting up because we were out with my favourite mare (actually a cousin, or stepsister, or something, anyway, also coincidentally born and raised at Holme Grove Stud).

But she must have given it some thought (and later, when the truth was discovered, felt *enormously* guilty) because not long after that she tried to give me a bit of time off.

Unfortunately, that was not looked upon favourably by the YOM, who considered holidaying horses to be detrimental to her hotel (and nobody saw the irony in that...) as they were considered more likely to play up. I'm not entirely sure I didn't compound that view with my behaviour, and it may have been at that time I earned the (I like to think affectionate) nickname Rodney (apparently a brave and intelligent character in something called *Only Fools and Horses*) amongst the B&B-ers, for being a bit of a plonker.

Before my antics got me made homeless, I was finally seen by the yard physio – thankfully a supremely respected and experienced horsewoman, who had previously given me the regular maintenance treatments us horses often benefit from when we have to put up with carrying even short humans about.

On this occasion the physio took one look at my back and refused to treat me until I had been seen by a vet as she was concerned there was more to my behaviour than simply tired muscles or the usual stiffness, which she would normally treat with her TENS machine and well-placed pushes and pulls and stretches.

A few days later the vet arrived and asked to see me move on the lunge, but I had by this time got, by my standards, a bit... ummmm... violent, I suppose you'd call it. It's not my normal nature to try to kick my human's head in, I assure you. I had grown a little fond of her, but in my defence I *hurt*. A *lot*. Thankfully for all concerned (yes, I aimed one at the vet's head too, to make sure he got the message), he soon called that little jaunt to a halt and X-rayed my back.

He immediately identified my problem. I had a condition called kissing spine, whereby two or more (in my case three, rather inconveniently just in the saddle area) spinous processes (the knobbly bits) are so close together that they touch and cause incredible pain, like a human experiences when they slip a disc. It's as serious a condition for a horse as it sounds. My poor human nearly went into meltdown (thankfully I didn't have a clue, still drooling happily under the standing sedative required to allow them to X-ray, dreaming of beating Totilas in my next Elementary test and getting another blue sash). You see, this wasn't the first horse she'd experienced with a kissing spine.

I can't believe at this most (literally) painful part of my memoirs we are going to unceremoniously drop my story and talk about someone else, but... oh, too late... how rude...

Gem

My human stumbled across Gem completely by accident.

A friend had asked my human to accompany her when she was going to try a horse she was potentially going to arrange to share. This was a 15.2hh bay Anglo Arab mare called Lady, somewhat quirky but hugely talented it turned out, but I'm getting ahead of myself.

The humans arrived at Lady's yard and tried to hide their horror at the blinking state of it. They genuinely looked at each other and said that they could just turn around and drive straight back out again. BHS approved, it was not. So many horses and ponies in patches of paddock vaguely and loosely electric-fenced, trampolines outside stable doors, toys and stuff just lying around everywhere, and to top it off, inevitably, my human's nemesis – kids – seemingly around every corner, but it turns out there were only three, all belonging to the queen of this patch of our beautiful kingdom, a woman that would unexpectedly become my human's good friend, Tania.

Anyway, they put on their game faces and were greeted by Tania, who then wheeled out a slightly wild-eyed Lady. Tania clambered on hat-less and in trainers, bombed round the unfenced patch of dirt they used as a school for a bit, while the kids chased away the loose ponies that wandered in to join the action, and then offered her to my human's increasingly terrified-looking friend to try. The friend, to her credit, did gingerly hop on and walked round for about two circuits without bursting into tears, before my human took pity and asked if she'd like her to try the mare instead and let her know if Lady felt like she might have the potential to become suitable, with a few lessons, perhaps (mainly said for Tania's benefit; it would clearly take more than a few lessons for this particular partnership to trot, let alone blossom). Looking like she might start crying instead now out of sheer relief, the friend slid off and my human mounted.

Now my human is most definitely no Charlotte Dujardin; she wouldn't know one end of a pirouette (she genuinely had to google how to spell it) from the other. Do pirouettes even have ends? They just go round and round… Anyway, a grand prix rider clearly she is not. However, she does have a bit of a knack for making a, shall we say, less obviously gifted horse look less like a camel and more like it wouldn't get laughed out of a dressage arena.

And the unsuspecting Lady got the full treatment. One minute she'd been steaming round, nose as high as the suspiciously tight martingale would allow, negotiating the corners like a motorbike doing the wall of death, the next minute she found herself floating along, flicking her toes, with a strangely submissive contact to the light rein. To say that Tania's jaw dropped would be no exaggeration. Her tearaway mare that to date had just galloped about a bit on hacks, suddenly looked... OK, maybe not a million dollars, but at least like she might not actually kill her next victim/rider.

Now our Tania was a canny lass, and it took her no more than a few seconds to remember that amongst that oddball assortment of ponies and youngsters lurking about the place, was her secret weapon, The One with Potential, the real deal, her Gem.

Gem was royally bred. Literally. Her grandad was the stallion Mars, a horse bred by the Queen herself. She was a 16.2hh five-year-old bred in the purple for eventing, or even pure dressage. She was proper. She and I would have made an excellent couple, truly an equine Posh and Becks – me all handsome and sporty and talented (I can hear the husband laughing; he'll be itching to point out the flaw, or in his eyes the proof, of my analogy: that Becks may not be best known for his high intelligence), while Gem would be the tall, slim, elegant and aptly named Posh by my side.

She didn't look it that day, though. She was skinny and scruffy and clueless. (The less generous would say that made her *exactly* like Posh.) Having seen what a half-decent (and only half, mind, let's not be giving her ideas above her station) rider could do for Lady (who the friend, you will not be surprised to hear, gave the offer of a share arrangement due consideration for at least two seconds, before thanking Tania but admitting maybe they weren't quite a perfect match), Tania asked my human if she would take a look at her youngster. Once reassured that she meant equine and not human youngster, she felt slightly obliged to agree to see it.

There was vague mention that Gem had been sent away to be backed when she was four, but details were suspiciously sketchy, and there was no evidence of that from the way she galloped about on the end of a lunge line during Tania's "demonstration". Given all the circumstances, when Tania asked her how much she might charge to bring on the youngster, my somewhat alarmed human thought of her usual rate, upped it a bit and then doubled that for good measure, confident in the knowledge there was no way it would be accepted.

Woops.

So, after laying a few ground rules about containing loose ponies, and loose kids, for that matter, and about feeding the mare enough for her to take a bit of light work, my human started down a road that would give her so many laughs, so much fun and experience and, ultimately, completely break her heart.

Turns out raising a young horse in a chaotic, noisy, messy environment, where kids literally crawl under and over said young horse at will, isn't actually such a bad thing after all. There wasn't much my human could do to startle her and Gem, possibly just grateful for some quiet time in the arena, was a pleasure to back/re-back (depending on who you believed), put on weight and developed from an ugly duckling into a beautiful swan in no time. She had an absolutely enormous jump in her, as well as naturally good, if not quite extravagant, paces. But most of all, she was sweet and gentle and always tried so hard. My human was hooked.

They were soon out wowing dressage judges and schooling round tracks. As was Lady! The tearaway mare, it turned out, was a delight to ride as long as my human avoided any more of leg aid whatsoever any stronger than the merest twitch of her calf muscle (no such restrictions with me, I might add; she can twitch like she's just been tasered, but I'm not shifting for anything unless I know I'll get a rather more convincing kick if I don't).

Lady was successful in the dressage ring, highlights including being placed at a hotly contested championships at Hickstead and being called over at the end of another test for a judge to ask her breeding as she was so taken with her. The story was a little different if my human forgot herself for a moment and actually used her little stumpies; the results certainly did not resemble dressage. And heaven forbid she carry a whip! Once she was *nearly* presented with her prize for winning a show-jumping class – a very beautiful leather crop, but Lady spotted it approaching and made it perfectly clear she was having none of it.

Mares, eh?

Lady also thoroughly enjoyed her XC. (*Why?* What *do* they see in all that hectic scampering and boinging?) Despite having never seen a XC fence in her previous twelve years, she whizzed round the riding club courses and BE Intro courses, and had scope for much higher. My human was convinced the mare had missed her calling in life as a really pretty smart eventer, but leg issues (I mean Lady's, not the stumpies) restricted her from venturing down that path in her teens.

Meanwhile, Gem was blossoming into a horse with huge potential. Her first year of competing saw many a dressage win, including an astronomical score of eighty-one per cent, and an eventing win. She won dressage championships at Hickstead and Oldencraig, and a fiercely competitive riding club qualifier. But she was no rosette machine; she could occasionally say "no" too. One such day saw her come last in her first test with a rather toe-curling fifty-two per cent, having basically refused to go forwards, preferring upwards, sometimes on four feet, sometimes on two. An hour later she won her next test with seventy-seven per cent.

I repeat: mares, eh?

Actually, despite that day coming very shortly before the championships wins, it had already rung alarm bells with my human, who just didn't feel like that was Gem just having an off moment. She was a genuine horse that had always tried for her rider. Apparently they say (not sure who "they" are, but they are clearly wrong; I am a gelding, after all) that you can't beat a good mare, and my human's opinion was that this was a good, kind and honest mare.

So, my human rode rather carefully at the championships, aware that Gem wasn't to be pushed but blissfully unaware that they would be her last competitions. What followed was Gem saying "no" more and more during her work at home and even out on hacks. All the usual checks were done – tack, teeth and back – then the vet checked her over, did lameness tests, considered ulcers, watched her being ridden and when she reared bolt upright, decided she was just trying it on and needed to be "ridden through it" (my human's least favourite phrase, as it usually involves either gritting her teeth to try and ignore an unsound horse or gritting her teeth while the horse performs low-flying acrobatics beneath – ideally – her, or both). The vet suggested that Gem was just at "that" age and stage.

So my human, to her later abject sorrow, kept on riding her, kept pushing, kept clinging on tight through whatever Gem threw at her until finally she said "no" herself and agreed with Tania they needed a second opinion.

The fateful day came and they took Gem for her referral appointment at the renowned Liphook Veterinary hospital, where a hugely respected and experienced vet watched my human ride her for all of about thirty seconds (and for the last time ever, it turned out), immediately halted proceedings and X-rayed her back. He found a horrendous and extensively damaged spine due to kissing spine, which he considered inoperable and untreatable. The only grain of hope he could offer, as the only alternative to immediate euthanasia, was simply to give the mare time – as in potentially years, for bones to fuse and damage to settle, as long as she remained pain-free while unridden. After what that kind and beautiful mare had given in the previous months, despite the agonising pain she must have been in at times, my human was categoric in her support of that and so, thankfully, Gem came home.

Meanwhile, my human had been completely unaware that Tania's marriage was breaking down and, to her absolute devastation, just a few months after Gem's diagnosis, and virtually overnight and without warning, Tania left the area completely, taking Gem, Lady and her numerous other horses with her. My human never saw any of them again.

Back to Me - At Last

So, it was with this backstory fresh in her mind and heart that my human heard the fateful words "kissing spine" again, this time – far more importantly – relating to me. Cue meltdown.

Before she was able to launch off into full-blown hysteria or threaten to throw herself off the stable roof (single-storey, probably would only have made a messy bloodstain on the car park and made the YOM shout at her), thankfully for all concerned, not least me (not that I was actually concerned at that moment – remember drooling, Totilas, sash, etc.), the vet proclaimed it entirely treatable. I "merely" had three "knobbly bits" that were just a little misshapen and so too close – no fusion, no bits that needed surgical intervention. Not a career-ending issue (ah well, I couldn't have it all).

He would simply inject into the spine (pardon me? He would *what*? *Where*? Oh, more sedation first, fantastic – maybe this time I'll beat Finbarr at a puissance and get a garland made of flowers) and that should remove the pain for six to twelve months before simply needing to be repeated.

And that is precisely what happened. Just like that. Pain-free.

I felt great and celebrated by tearing round my field in a most un-dressage-like manner.

And damaged a ligament in my left foreleg.

My human was beside herself. Don't think the YOM was impressed either; even she couldn't insist or guilt-trip my human into keeping me in any sort of work. I was to be a gentlemen of leisure for months, my absolutely favourite type of life but absolutely not her favourite type of "guest". It was at this point we were politely asked to leave. My ego remains, to this day, more than a little bruised as the YOM made it unnecessarily and painstakingly clear that it wasn't personal against my human, and that *she* was welcome back to the horse hotel any time... I, however, somewhat less so. I'm pretty sure the phrase "over my dead body" was used. I'm not sure whose dead body she was referring to, but, regardless, I don't think I came out of the discussion well.

However, once again my human managed a stay of execution as she had a little nugget of information she shared with the YOM – that, despite the outrageous price of any property in the area with just enough land to so much as tether a goat, she and her soon-to-be ex-husband (I'll come to that) were in the process of buying a tiny house with a few acres and stables, having made a bit of a killing on developing their own property, which they were in the middle of selling. So if the YOM could just be kind enough and patient enough (grovel, grovel) to bear with her while the sale and purchase went through, although it may take a couple of months or more, then it would save me the trauma of changing yards twice in a short time (and she knows how I feel about change).

Against all odds, the YOM relented (she must have *really* liked my human) and I was banished to a field further down the lane, with the other main DIY-er for company, so my I'm-not-in-work-hurrah antics didn't have to be witnessed.

All good then, yes?

No.

You might be wondering why my human would be buying a house with her soon-to-be ex-husband? Well, it wasn't quite like that. When they *started* the purchase (apparently these things can drag on for many months, as did this one – fortuitously, as it turned out), they weren't soon-to-be exes, despite her innermost wishes. However, her innermost wishes finally became outermost, and, over many months, they talked, avoided, stuck their heads in the sand, talked some more (I know all this because she would come and sit in the field and tell me all about it, whether I wanted to hear it or not – thankfully not stopping me from grazing, though, so frankly I'm surprised I remember any of it), all while their house sale and purchase were rumbling along.

Finally, and thankfully, if only for my digestion, their house sale fell through and so they had to abandon the house-with-stables purchase. While this avoided them being bound together in a whole new situation – which my human had realised had gone from being a life-long dream of having her horse at home to being a dreaded nightmare of being trapped, even more than she already was, in the company of someone unpleasant – it didn't do the safety of my tenure at my hotel any good at all.

The YOM's patience, already stretched beyond all previously known records, not unexpectedly, snapped.

My human didn't even get time to do the research/spreadsheet thing in the search for my next abode. A few hasty phone calls and a very kind offer from a lady who recognised a dire situation and a human at her limits, to let me go and stay as a livery at her stud farm, saw my next, rather hasty, move.

Stud Life

Yeeaaahhhh, baby, I'm a stud. Livin' the dream! C'mon, ladies, let the bees see the honey...

I'm so sorry, not entirely sure what came over me – must be all the testosterone raging around the barn.

I have to say I was impressed when I arrived, my human did good at finding this hotel. My new stable is... well... new! A brand-new, beautiful, purpose-built barn with six indoor stables. My neigh-bours (pardon the pun) include a PRE stallion who qualified for the Olympics (presumably at dressage and not at being a stallion – didn't think *that* was an Olympic sport) and another ridiculously handsome young stallion. I'm back on the full hotel service – B&B-ers need not apply here – and my staff seem very pleasant. Outside are rolling fields of mares and foals just enjoying life and I have my own day paddock, subject to seemly social distancing.

To be honest, I'm not one hundred per cent on the details of what my duties involve now I'm "a stud", but the other chaps here seem pretty enthusiastic about it.

My human just rolls her eyes quite a lot and tells me to get over myself whenever I try to catch the eyes of the ladies, but she needn't worry; for some inexplicable reason they don't seem the slightest bit interested in me – I really can't understand it. Probably just playing hard to get.

Mares, eh?

So, do we all get to live happily ever after *this* time?

Of course not, where would be the fun (or the story) in that?

For starters, my human…

Despite my "stumpy" references, I'm only commenting on the nature of her vertical challenge, not the horizontal element. I do count myself lucky that I haven't been saddled with (gosh, all these clever puns, I'm so funny) a gargantuan human; she's never actually been particularly heavy, to be fair to the old girl. Solid, maybe, but not heavy.

But over recent months I had noticed that my load was lightening somewhat. In fact, now I look at her properly I'm beginning to think she could do with a decent feed, perhaps some fresh grass, or maybe she just needs worming. If our roles were reversed and she were the noble horse and I the humble human, I'm pretty sure I wouldn't turn her out without a rug on in case someone spotted her and thought she was some awful case of neglect and called in the RSPCA. Yep, she was definitely getting a bit ribby.

Having listened to all her tales of woe on our hacks, what I began to realise was that it's not just us horses that suffer from stress-related issues. While I hadn't yet caught her pacing up and down a fence-line, it was surely only a matter of time. Turns out the whole lead up to and finally the actual act of separation from The Ex had taken its toll on her. Her normally self-confessed dreadfully greedy appetite and love of all the wrong foods had abandoned her, and her weight plummeted. Not necessarily a bad thing to begin with (sorry, human, but the truth hurts, and that first stone dropped got you from a 3.5 to a 3 on the horsey body condition scoring chart).

It was the weight loss beyond that which took its toll.

Now due to said normal appetite, my human had generally always been pretty dismissive of other humans, usually female, usually half her age, who wailed about being "too slim". "Oh, poor them," she'd sarcastically mutter, "must be awful, really hellish." An attitude probably not helped when said wailing was usually undertaken on social media, accompanied by a photo of the "too slim" young thing looking lithe and stunning in some miniscule outfit that would make my human look like one of the *Fat Slag* cartoon characters. She wasn't bitter, or jealous, you understand, just utterly scathing.

However, she started to have some unexpected sympathy with the genuine amongst these young waifs when her own weight, unintentionally, went so far south. By which I mean the numbers kept dropping, as opposed to the other meaning of "the weight going south" more normally experienced by someone, let's say slightly post-prime in years, such as her good self.

While there was a barely suppressed smugness at her having to keep going out to buy the next size down in jeans, when she reached a size 6 skinny jean because she could slip off the size 8s without undoing the zip, even she could see it really wasn't pretty.

And along with that, she lost strength and robustness, more importantly was unable to school me properly, if at all, and, inevitably, fell ill. There followed a very bleak time in which her visits to see me became more and more sporadic, and even when she did she'd often only lunge me, one-handedly and slightly hunched over, with the other arm clutched across her midriff, somehow trying to hold in the pain. At her worst moment she had pleurisy, bronchitis and tonsillitis all at the same time and could barely stand, once even failing to do that, collapsing outside my stable. Frankly, if she'd been a horse... Know what I'm saying?

But never mind about her; far more importantly, what about me? With only minimum work, if you could call it that, and minimum turnout, as it was winter by now – you know what's coming, don't you? Of course, I became unsettled – both in the stable and in the field. It wasn't my fault, naturally, but there had been so much change, and my human was being weird, or just wasn't around. Apparently, she couldn't afford to pay the yard dressage rider to work me because she found herself paying not only the full mortgage on the ex-marital home (because the vile ex refused to pay a penny, despite living there on his own) while they were still trying to sell it after several lengthy almost-sales fell through, but also the rent on her own home. Oh, and my not-entirely-inexpensive hotel bills too. No wonder she didn't eat much.

My "being a tit" (not my words, you'll not be surprised to learn) in the stable meant I disturbed the stallions, which was not only socially frowned upon but categorically Not Allowed. With embarrassing haste I was moved from the Presidential Suite to an Economy room, a dark, gloomy indoor stable in an older waiting-to-be-renovated barn, with just a mare I'd never met for company.

That did not help my behaviour.

To my shame, I had escalated from being "a tit" to being "a dangerous moron", and my human struggled, in her pathetically weakened state, to so much as enter my stable at times, let alone attempt to do anything with me to help bring me down. It was a vicious circle. And guess what? On the occasions I was turned out, I was fence-pacing/mud-making again! Who knew!

Inevitably, and ultimately thankfully, before anybody got hurt, the stud owner suggested, in the kindest possible way, to my human that "it wasn't really working"… for anybody… having me there. My human made the most feeble attempts (compared to previous extensive research, visits, spreadsheets, etc.) to find me an emergency new home, and two days after Christmas I found myself shunted off to who-knew-where this time.

Happy Christmas?

Ah yes, that fateful day. While I was fence-pacing/stable-trashing and generally having a hellish time, it turned out my human's Christmas was a whole lot worse.

You see, she had met a new chap and he visited her on Christmas morning, which was nice.

Unfortunately, the vile ex decided to pop by too, categorically uninvited and unwanted, and it was not nice.

On sight of another car outside my human's home, he proceeded to break in and violently assault my human's new friend, a gentleman and a gentle man, who had done nothing wrong and who ended up, days later, having surgery to rebuild his shattered face.

My human was horrified, naturally. The ex left, after making all sorts of threats against her, the friend and even me. He then returned a few minutes later with a friend of his own and took my human's car so she was left feeling like a sitting duck, totally vulnerable to a return visit.

Thankfully her parents swooped in and collected her, and then her ridiculously generous sister lent my human her own car so she could still work, and escape from her own home if needs be, and, most importantly, visit me.

Over the following days and weeks she discovered how amazing and true her friends were (mostly!). While the ex was contacting pretty much anyone they'd ever met, including her family and their mutual friends, to tell them all sorts of wild (and entirely fictitious) stories about her, all but one family of friends chose to trust that the Ali they had known for many years was indeed exactly the honest, trustworthy, solid person they knew, and chose not to believe the outrageous shenanigans they were being told. Some, much later, told her that they wondered if some of the tales might be true but had only thought, rather hilariously, "Good for her," or, more to the point, "Nothing to do with me," and carried on supporting her regardless. You see, the ex had rather shot himself in the foot unleashing such a violent assault on an innocent party and in a place he had no business being (details curiously missing from his tales) and thereby revealing his true nature.

Inevitably, the new chap kept his distance somewhat for a time, while he healed in many ways. But, happily for my human, it turned out he's not someone who takes well to being told what he can and can't do. Especially by a bully. Showing admirable bravery and strength of character, he returned to her side and carved his place there to face whatever challenges were thrown their way.

I rather like to think that this episode, rather than push them apart, actually put them on the path to their later marriage. See, *someone* eventually gets to live happily ever after!

My Happy Place

So, under a bit of a dark cloud in many ways, I was moved to my new home a couple of days after the physical and emotional battering of a Christmas better suited to an episode of *EastEnders*.

A wonderful friend (Victoria, of the Bumble episode) offered a towing service for my trailer, on account of the generous sister's little Astra not exactly being up to the job, and in the absence of my human's AWOL Shogun. (Side note, the Shogun was returned to her some months later, on the day after its MOT expired!) Victoria also ended up lifting rather a lot of tack, rugs, metal feed bins and boxes upon boxes of the equine detritus that my human had collected over the years, while my human shuffled about, feebly repeating, "Sorry," over and over. A wonderful friend indeed.

As mentioned, this particular hotel was a really rather lastminute.com booking, being found under more than a little pressure and when my human was far from being at her best. She wasn't convinced that this would be for any more than a short vacation, until she found something maybe more suitable, given a bit more time and focus. Her concern was chiefly that the hotel was managed by an extraordinarily young lady (OK, I know anyone under the age of thirty looked about twelve to her, but still…). How could such a "child" (mid-twenties, actually) possibly have the experience to take proper care of such a fine steed as myself?

Turns out she could.

In spades.

Yes, the lovely Freddie was an absolute breath of fresh air for my, at that time, somewhat damaged human, and for me too. She not only tolerated my "character"; she found ways to minimise its effects. She was the first to identify me as "OCD" and took the time and trouble to manage my "disorder". That's not to say she never called me a tit or a moron, as had several yard managers before her, but she was ever-cheerful, exceptionally hard-working and a gifted and sensitive horsewoman. She, and the lovely friendly liveries, unwittingly provided a much-needed convalescing environment for both horse and human.

The measure of Freddie was the way she shrugged off an early, rather ominous, visit to the stables from the ex, who wanted all to be aware he knew exactly where I was should he wish to carry out any of his threats. Thankfully, though, that was the last I ever had to see of him. Never did take to him.

Our lives were turned around from this moment on, for the better. It is a fact that, like it or not, my human's psychological well-being is intrinsically linked to my own. I relaxed into my new surroundings, so she could relax a little. I sensed she was no longer in such a dark place and I became manageable and ride-able, so as she grew in strength again, from that ridiculous six stone and something weed, we enjoyed our rides and work. The more these happy events occurred, the stronger and happier she got, and so the more we rode, and the happier and more relaxed I got, and so it went on.

And we were in the presence of dressage royalty on the yard. None other than international dressage rider Amy Stovold kept her young superstar-in-the-making Bo-Bo there. I'm not sure I entirely approved of the way my human looked with such awe at him strutting his fancy-pants stuff in the arena. I was also concerned (rightly so, as it turned out) when Amy agreed to give us some training.

That sounded like hard work.

And, oh boy, it was. Not just each lesson but then the homework my human would do in between. Amy had spotted, within a millisecond of watching us work, that the effort ratio was ninety per cent human to ten per cent horse – in other words, in my eyes, perfect.

Apparently not.

And so years of my training my human to push, lift, kick, carry and strain for every stride was undone. My human had become a fan of this new method. Me… less so.

Within a few months we were back out at pony parties, and at our first competition in eighteen months, after injuries and so much stress, I won our first class.

The new chap/husband-to-be-although-he-had-no-idea-at-the-time was there to witness her happy tears at the scoreboard, and perhaps it struck him at that point just how much I meant to my human and that we came as a pair. Once again, testament to his strength of character (or perhaps lack of crystal ball to see what a large part of *his* life I would become) that he didn't just immediately run for the hills. I wonder if since he has wished he had... I know at times he's wished that I had, or indeed, still would.

I continued to have my annual injections for my kissing spine, which worked like magic every time, and apart from my usual regular physio treatments to keep me in tip-top shape, I think I was pretty low maintenance (why is my human making such a strange snorting noise?).

Well, I couldn't let that continue indefinitely. I've never regarded myself as a low-maintenance kind of guy and she often refers to me as a princess which, while I (pretend to) have issue with the gender, I can't disagree with the sentiment.

And so our yard trip to the beach came to pass.

All the horses and riders bundled onto a convoy of trailers, making it look like the circus was coming to town (no prizes for guessing who was marked down as chief clown by the end of the day), drove for an hour or so to the coast and unloaded at the field beside the beach at Ferring.

I had never been to a beach before and was bewildered as to why the whole yard would come to a dressage show with me, so I behaved like a bit of a giraffe while she was getting me ready. However, she knows me so well, and I warmed up and calmed down on the grass field by doing lots of lovely, comforting safe circles before we all headed for the shore. There was a weird pebbly slippy slidey downhill bit, which I didn't approve of (not dressage, darling), but then we got to a sandy bit, which wasn't dissimilar to some arenas I've been in, so I deemed that acceptable. Unfortunately, some fool had left the plug in and this particular arena was flooded as far as the eye could see. I was terribly brave (more snorting) and went in all the way up to my knees (after letting some others lead the way to check its safety before being silly enough to risk myself, much like royalty might allow their minions to sample food so that said minions get poisoned instead of the, in this case, prince(ss). But no one was attacked by a shark or alligator, so in I plunged. I say plunged; it was more like my "wearing boots" walk, but the point is I went in, OK?).

A lovely time was had by all, and we returned to the trailers triumphant from our delightful evening. My human was just untacking me when I saw *it*… the *thing*… it was a huge, buzzy, darting *bug*, like a horse fly on steroids – huge it was, enormous, definitely a horse-killer.

So I legged it.

Well, I tried to leg it, but that blinking, stubborn little human clung on to my headcollar like a Kardashian to her stylist in a storm. All I succeeded in doing was flinging my back end round in a huge half circle before (to my abject embarrassment) falling over my feet and rather publicly crashing onto my bottom. I tried to style it out by leaping up again in what definitely would have looked like one unbroken elegant ballet move, hoping no one had noticed, but inevitably, the one time I *didn't* want to be centre of attention, of course all eyes were on me.

However, tough and brave fellow that I am (really, snorting is so un-ladylike), I trotted up sound after my little incident and, hoping that would be the end of it, I loaded a little sheepishly and rather gratefully on my trailer and off home the convoy went (actually via a drive-through Maccy-D's, I seem to recall, which must have been quite a sight – and, now I come to think of it, I never did get my veggie burger).

Apart from that, all was well.

Till the next day.

When, upon inspecting my divine, if bruised, bottom, my human noticed a small swelling. Rolling her eyes, she told me that wouldn't be enough to get a day off and we had a lovely, reassuring safe schooling session, with no flooded arenas or low-flying horse-eating insects of doom.

Needless to say, the small swelling grew. And grew. Until even my ever-tight (sorry, "experienced") human thought a vet should check it over. The vet came and pronounced it the biggest haematoma she'd ever seen. It was by now bigger than a dinner plate in width and really rather bulging and wobbly. To my human's alarm the vet also said there's absolutely nothing to be done with it until it had stopped growing, as interfering with it before then would only mean it would grow back to run its full course. In fact, the best thing to do was nothing; they are apparently best left alone to reabsorb and simply disappear by themselves.

It was so big and wobbly that the vet even said to avoid exercise (I do love vets, such wisdom) because it would at the very least be uncomfortable for me (imagine jumping up and down with the most enormous fluid-filled boil on your derriere), and at worst cause soft tissue damage.

Suffice it to say I strung this one out for aaaaages; it got me quite the summer holiday. When it had seemed to stop growing the vet revisited but said we should continue to wait to see if it would go naturally, as intervention wasn't always successful and came with its own risks. Finally, after waiting (impatiently watching the summer slide by on her side, blissfully watching the summer slide by on mine), it was arranged for the vet to come and "lance" it.

Now I wasn't entirely sure what that meant, but, as with so many vet's visits, the first thing that happened was that I was sedated and sent off into la-la land, so, frankly, I really didn't care. My human wasn't entirely sure what the procedure involved either but got an idea when the vet asked for a large bucket, which she then placed on the floor below my bump and told my human to stand back. Those of a nervous disposition or with a delicate tummy should probably skip the next bit.

With a scalpel, and at a stretched arm's length, the vet made a small incision. The pressure release and sheer size of the haematoma meant the most hideously vast quantity of revolting fluid shot out of that small incision like water from a hose with a thumb half over the end. Unfortunately, an unsuspecting young human at that precise moment happened to pop her head over the stable door to say hi, to be met with what looked like the grand finale scene from *The Chainsaw Horse Massacre*, so she turned green and bid a hasty retreat, making gagging noises.

Thankfully, my human was either made of sterner stuff or was too shocked to move, as she stayed put, merely shifting the filling bucket to catch it all as necessary. Even the vet seemed pretty impressed when she inspected the contents of the bucket once the hose had reduced to a drip.

The vet then, with a suspicious glint in her eye and far too much pleasure at sharing such a gory task, explained to her that my human would have to flush out the cavity daily, through the incision, which the vet would leave open for that purpose, to ensure all the blood clots and potential sources of infection or problems were removed before the cavity healed. Game enough, my human took on all the instructions and equipment and arrived at my stable the next day to do just that.

It was only at that point that she realised that I, of course, was now not sedated. The penny dropped at why the vet had such a glint in her eye. My human was to approach my kicking end with numerous syringes of sterile water, insert them into an open wound and generally have a jolly good rummage about the cavity to flush out any gunky bits.

Really?

Yes, actually, really. That is exactly what happened. And, once again, no one was killed.

On her first attempt at the deed, my human, braced for a brutal but probably mercifully quick death, soon discovered, to both of our hearty relief, that I, bizarrely, rather liked it. It was like have an itch scratched. She didn't have to ply me with drugs, or herself with alcohol, in preparation. I stood like a rock every time she did it, even the day she spotted something white-ish sticking out of the wound, when she thought I'd managed to get a bit of shaving from my bedding in it and went to pull it out.

She struggled, mind, had to get her fingernails right in to get hold of it, and then she pulled… and pulled… and turned out it wasn't a shaving at all; it was like a grey elastic band. It just kept coming, and coming, to the point where she thought she'd made an horrific mistake and expected my (allegedly) teeny tiny brain to pop out of the hole like a cork from a champagne bottle (not that she could remember what that sounds like – strictly in the Prosecco set, that one).

Anyway, at about the point where she was beginning to wonder if she shouldn't start trying to stuff it all back in, the end of the gooey grey mass popped out of the hole and plopped on the floor at the very same time as the poor young human who had previously, just a few days before, briefly witnessed *The Chainsaw Horse Massacre* scene, skipped happily and obliviously round the corner of the yard to witness my human apparently trying to turn me inside out, bit by bit.

I think she actually screamed this time.

Ignoring (glad she had her priorities right) the traumatisation and surely permanent emotional damage done to an innocent girl my, by now, really rather concerned human, ingeniously took a photo of the offending article and messaged it to the vet, who to her giddy relief reassured her that it was just an old blood clot and that it was excellent that it was out and not in. Relief all round – time perhaps to hear that Prosecco cork popping, after all.

And so time passed contentedly by: hacking out with our new friends, competing successfully and generally finding our happy place in the world.

Well, *that* wasn't going to last, was it? Thankfully it wasn't *me* this time that triggered a move.

It's a Dog's Life

As time passed happily by, my human and her boyfriend were now living together with his two gorgeous German Shepherds.

Seems a bit unfair that the dogs get to go home with them both while I get left behind to fend for myself at some hotel, but as "fending for myself" consists of breakfast in bed every day, having my clothes for the day selected from my extensive wardrobe to suit my very specific requirements depending on forecast temperature/precipitation/wind speed, followed by play time in the paddocks with my friends leaving the staff to sort out my, frankly disgusting, bedroom, a visit from the human for some fuss and a ride in the afternoon, then a Deliveroo every night with snacks for throughout the evening, I managed to bravely put up with my lot.

But apparently those dogs have a lot to answer for. You see, my human and her ex had a German Shepherd too, who was delightful but stark-raving bonkers, in a zebedee-bouncy ridiculously over-friendly brain-the-size-of-a-pea kind of way, all tail and tongue. So, the fateful decision was made to take her to a German Shepherds-only-need-apply obedience class every week.

These classes were held in a church hall and I shudder at the thought of all that barking and chaos in such a cavernous echoey place. I prefer the reverent hushed-tones of the dressage warm-up (unless some *birk* has brought their screeching trainer to stand in the gateway, booming right across the 100m warm-up at their increasingly quivering wreck of a doomed pupil, punctuating conflicting instructions with, "Ya, gud," to confirm to all unfortunately forced to listen that she is German-trained, i.e. watched a YouTube video by someone with an un-pronounceable name).

I was surprised to learn how many not-quite (or indeed, not at all) obedient GSDs regularly attended such classes, from puppies to elderly dogs who really should have known better (or did in fact know better but chose to ignore it and carry on enjoying themselves. My human says she's known a few horses like that, while looking at me darkly).

This could easily have descended into three hours of Monday-night mayhem, save for one beacon of sanity and hope, the mighty force that was the club's human leader, the all-powerful, all-seeing and all-knowing Sandra, or She Who Must Be Obeyed, as she was known to dogs and humans alike.

Now, SWMBO was not mighty in stature, but woe betide two legs or four underestimating the power that she beheld to (largely) quiet a hall of excited, barking, plunging beasts (and their dogs) and focus them all on the highly technical art of walking to heel (honestly, I mastered that years ago, but, to be fair, I'm still struggling with "stay" and a command to "sit" is merely responded to with a raised eyebrow and a yawn, much like some of the dogs in class, and as for "fetch", well, you know what you can do with that command).

I'd like to say that my human and her husband-to-be's eyes met over a crowded, noisy, chaotic room, and sparks flew, angels sang and their futures were written in the stars at that moment. But I suspect it was rather more that his glance slid straight to her dog bouncing on the end of its lead like Tigger on LSD, thinking that a room full of excited cousins looked like *awesome* fun, and thought, "Hope that bonkers mutt stays away from mine, it'll set him off," while my human took one look round the room and tried to find a corner to hide in.

There followed several months of training under the beady eye of SWMBO, and matters progressed. When I say "matters" I mean their dogs' training; there was no scope for any other sort of shenanigans, or frankly any anything, unless instructed by Their Great Leader. However, once they both found themselves single, a dog walk (naturally) was suggested... and the rest, as they say, is history...

So, they had begun living together in my human's rented house until the landlords decided they wanted to sell the property and gave her notice to leave (now she knows how it feels). Concerned at trying to find another rental property that would accept two big dogs, the humans ended up moving into a place that he and his dogs had previously stayed in, owned by none other than SWMBO, who had become a good friend of his.

Now this place, affectionately known as The Shack, was, to be kind, not in tip-top condition.

It was a demolition job. Literally.

It had lain largely empty for a few years since its elderly occupants had passed away, and, being of entirely timber construction (basically it was a big shed – a two-bed stable, if you will), it was damp and rotten. Frankly, I wouldn't have entertained the notion of residing in it myself; if I leant on a wall to have a good scratch I may have flattened it anyway. It was to be demolished and the site developed.

However, being on the site next to SWMBO's own beautiful old cottage, it was set in the most delightful gardens still maintained by a gardener, at the end of a grassy rural lane, so it was the most charming little shack, truly an idyllic garden shed set in paradise.

Such paradise, though, had never seen such frivolous luxuries as central heating, double glazing, a shower or a washing machine. It really was a step back in time.

This didn't stop the intrepid humans, though. Over one long Easter weekend (during which I had a lovely rest – how marvellous) they stripped out old damp furniture, carpets and curtains, tore down/up rotten walls and floors and replaced them, painted every room white (brightening and freshening and, not to forget, covering the mould), rigged up a shower and installed a washing machine, and scrubbed and cleaned everywhere. By the end of four long, exhausting (not for me!) days, The Shack had not only stepped into the twentieth century but also become a home again.

It was supposed to be a temporary fix for just a few spring and summer months until they found somewhere to buy. But they loved their new home so much that, in time, their now-neighbour SWMBO ridiculously generously offered to sell them it, instead of her developing it. Pretty sure it was only so that her own four (yes, *four*!) German Shepherds could continue to play "chase" up and down the connecting hedge line, with my humans' two dogs, as they did at every opportunity. Now, do tell, why is it deemed entertaining and "play" when dogs run up and down a fence-line but "destructive" and "moronic" when a horse does it? On second thoughts, don't answer that.

So, the humans set about trying to raise finance to purchase The Shack. Now while they were offered, subject to survey, a sufficiently eye-watering won't-retire-till-I'm-eighty mortgage to afford the purchase and subsequent somewhat scaled-down development from SWMBO's original plans, when it came to said survey (much like a vetting, as I understand it), the house-vet actually had the tenacity to laugh at their proposal. He visited The Shack, declared it unfit for habitation (bit rude, albeit probably technically true) and so it resoundingly failed the vetting (you know the drill – only one good leg will cost you more in vets' fees in the first year than you spend buying it, a total money pit – coincidentally *exactly* what the vet said about the mighty eventer Rubbish when my human had him vetted).

Unfortunately, the humans couldn't buy The Shack regardless of vetting, like my human did with Rubbish (to then have ten incredible storming years with him), as the lenders declared that they were really only buying a plot of land – no housey, no money.

It was after this gutting news that my humans went away for their second holiday to the Scottish Highlands. They had previously holidayed there and found the space, peace and natural beauty just staggering. All sounds a bit chilly to me; don't they have *snow* up there? I'm more of a lazing by the pool in the sun kind of chap, but each to their own. I suppose if *everyone* liked it cold and rainy then the Highlands wouldn't be so spacious, peaceful and naturally beautiful, so I guess it kind of works out about right for everyone (except me, so it would turn out).

You Want
to Live Where?
(More importantly,
you want *me* to live where?)

While on holiday, they did apparently what most people do on holiday – yes, declared that such was their deep and ever-lasting love for the destination that one day, far into the future, they would go and live there, maybe when they retired. Although, judging by the prospect of being mortgaged until they were into their dotage, it was a strong possibility they wouldn't even remember where the Highlands were by then, let alone why they wanted to live there.

However, desperately sadly, while away they got news that his father was diagnosed with terminal cancer, which rather put them in a different place mentally. Literally overnight their dream of one day heading off to spend their sunset years in some rugged and remote spot on the side of a mountain came to an abrupt end.

And was replaced with a somewhat more short-term idea.

Their thinking had been given the proverbial kick up the derriere, and they realised that life could, sadly for some, literally be too short, that they didn't know what the future might hold for them too, that they may not get the chance to be able to realise their dreams if all they did was dream. They had to act.

Now my human, as I may have mentioned, is one for careful research, planning and spreadsheets. What I may not have mentioned, and what may not be apparent from events of the previous couple of years, is that she, just like me, isn't a great one for change. And that revelation after all the stick I've had for being change-averse! And while she doesn't necessarily balk at a moved pole in the school, or a different colour leaf, I have trained her over the years to, on spotting such monsters, sit up, shorten her reins and so, yes, reacting to change herself!

So, this potentially gargantuan, sweeping change of her entire life was not considered lightly. I'm not sure that it would have been considered at all if her employers hadn't supported her preposterous plan. You see, she really rather liked her job in Surrey – her bosses, her colleagues, even some of the clients. She also (once again, rather like my good self) likes stability, and for her that included remaining with the same firm she had been with for eighteen years (told you, change-averse) and being as confident as anyone can be that she wouldn't be out of a job. She was worried that a) there weren't many jobs available half-way up a mountain, and b) that she would move to a stunning location only to spend her days commuting to, and working in, an office much like any other.

So, while still on holiday, she came up with the genius idea that she could continue to work for her Reigate firm but just mostly work from home. In the Highlands.

So it was with this outlandish notion – which, the more she thought about it the more she realised no employer would agree to because... well... why would they? – that she returned to work from her holiday and approached one of her two bosses, more nervously than I approach a stable from which I can hear the sound of clippers warming up. To her astonishment the proposal wasn't met with hysterical laughter, or dismissed as the rantings of a woman who had clearly suffered from hypothermia or frost-bite on the brain; it was met with the words, "Well, we don't want to lose you," and a promise to discuss with the other boss.

And he agreed!

To her total disbelief, and surprising lack of nervousness, she had the thumbs-up to go and live in the Highlands and work from home there, as long as she could spend a week or so a month back at the office in Reigate to catch up and pick up and drop off files.

It was only then that she allowed herself to start her online property search. To begin with, the search parameters were pretty broad – the area being "Highlands", so that's ten thousand square miles, to which they added Aberdeenshire for good measure, another 2,500 square miles, put in their price range and added "rural" and "detached" (because they prefer animals to people), and that brought up over two thousand properties.

On scrolling through the many, many screens of properties, it soon dawned on her just how vast the price difference was between Surrey and their chosen remote areas of the Highlands. Their budget allowed them to consider some huge and beautiful houses. However, she soon dismissed the idea of buying a small hotel or ten-bedroom house on the basis of practicality, i.e. her penchant for house-cleaning is about as strong as it is for tack-cleaning, and she was shuddering as she imagined all that dusting and hoovering. Literally having one of those nightmares where you run frantically, but apparently through glue and without appearing to move forward, down an endless corridor of doors and can't find your way out, only now, to make it truly terrifying, she's pushing a hoover too. She also reminded herself that while they wanted to go somewhere with enough space around them to get away from hordes of people, they didn't also actually want to get away from each other by having five bedrooms each – they weren't married, after all!

Hmmmm, how to narrow the search? Well, then she started to consider splitting their budget between a nice, but somewhat less grand than the castles they had been looking at, Highlands home and a teeny tiny studio flat near the Reigate office for her to stay in when down south, which would probably cost more.

She then (about time too) remembered she had a fine and noble (and allegedly pain in the proverbial) horse to house, and the dilemmas multiplied (I seem to have that effect). Should I stay at Freddie's, where I was settled and safe, for her to see me for a week a month? Or should she cart me off to Scotland and risk me getting thrown off of yards up there? What if I didn't settle anywhere? Would anyone tolerate me and manage me as well as Freddie? Do they even have livery yards half-way up a mountain? Or do they just sling their Highland ponies out on the side of said mountain? Just how many layers of rugs is it possible for a horse to wear before one false move and he turns into an equine snowball? I could see this whole venture disappearing into a fog of stress and fear of worst-case scenarios.

Finally (and she reckons she's the intelligent one of us), the penny dropped. An equestrian Highlands property! With those prices they could afford one! That narrowed the search somewhat and, once they ruled out the west coast (too rainy, no grazing on account of all those mountains) and ruled out anywhere more than a ninety-minute drive to an airport for her monthly commute, they focussed on areas loosely around Inverness.

The possibilities she found online soon had them booking a four-day twelve-property-viewing trip. This was a trip planned with military precision (and I thought that was reserved for dressage show preparation) – flights, car hire, three nights in different hotels to put them in the right area for the first viewing each morning, the viewings organised with a dozen different agents in a specific order of day and time depending on geographical location and travel time between each – the spreadsheets went into overdrive; she was in her element.

The day of departure for the viewing trip soon arrived and the first potential spanner in the works had to be addressed. You see, my human, not quite as simple to manage as she likes to think (and looking more and more like she is as "quirky" as my good self), has a terrible fear of flying.

To be fair, I can see her point. Why would anyone want to get into a big metal tube, whose wings are filled with highly flammable liquid, with a herd of other people, and which is then shot at great speed into the sky in the hands of a complete stranger? I would say that her fear is as justified and sensible as my fear of cables... They are often attached to clippers, need I say more?

She has not only the fear of flying but also gets travel sick, a really top combination for someone considering commuting by plane every month. It would be like me planning to get clipped while eating lawn mowing clippings every few weeks, and, let me tell you, that is *never* fluffing happening.

So the flight took off. There were tears; there was an ashen face – and that was just him as she gripped his hand so tightly – but just an hour and twenty minutes later they touched down, in bonny Scotland, and in one piece (literally, she was still gripping him so tightly she wouldn't let go) to commence house-shopping manoeuvres.

After each viewing, notes were religiously taken lest they get to the end of each day in a jumble of confused thoughts about views, grazing quality, refurbishment costs, hacking options, neighbours, etc., etc. A few properties were dismissed pretty quickly, but after the four-day trip, seven of the twelve were still in contention! Of course, a second viewing was not immediately possible and so, once back home, she spent many happy hours poring over notes, spreadsheets and property brochures.

An unplanned-for addition to the list of factors to consider was that many of the properties, by virtue of most of them having acreage and barns, also either already had, or had realistic potential for, additional holiday accommodation. This would allow them to supplement their income with not insignificant holiday rental income. More cleaning, though.

Those properties on the short list were hugely varied. From an impressive hill-top house with staggering views and stone-built steading already part-converted to accommodation, but with "only" an acre of land, to a stunning and large contemporary home on a hillside, with ten acres of (partly marshy) grazing and limited hacking.

But there were two properties that they were most taken with, and which they did return to for second viewings on a Christmas trip back up to the Highlands. The first was a fifty-acre (crikey!) mini-farm with not just one but two traditional stone-built cottages, the largest of which had a huge and stunning open-plan kitchen/ living space complete with wall of windows looking over the land and up to the mountains beyond. But the combination of the odd upstairs arrangement (the main cottage had two sets of stairs to some odd rooms) and the potential cost for the much-needed updating of the second cottage and conversion of barns to stables, plus the addition of the compulsory arena to make me feel at home, put this into second place.

And the winner was… drum roll, please… inevitably, the first property they viewed originally. Turns out house-shopping with my human is much like clothes-shopping and shoe-shopping with her (but thankfully not horse-shopping) – she knows what she wants, knows where to get it, goes there, likes what she sees, doesn't buy it, goes to every other potential place to look at lots of similar items in the full knowledge she will likely return to the first place and buy there. Which is exactly what happened in Scotland.

Their property of choice required a little bit of vision, being in need of more than a little TLC, but had the potential to be really rather special. As it stood, it was a seven-bedroom house, kind of split in two, half of which hadn't been occupied for a while, with numerous barns, stables and outbuildings, an overgrown small arena and sixteen acres, scruffily and loosely fenced, set at the end of a farm lane, directly onto an endless sandy beach with a forest beside and views up to mountains over the firth. For her it was the property version of Gem – something that needed rescuing and love and effort, with the potential to be incredible and to give back ten-fold what was put in. Her only hope was that it didn't also end in tears…

So on Christmas Eve they returned there, ignored normal protocol for house-buying in Scotland whereby offers are to be made via solicitors and shook hands on a price with the owner. The deal was done!

And, as if that wasn't enough excitement, on Christmas Day they got engaged! I'd like to say that he popped the question, but actually he got the dogs to do it. He got each of them in turn to present her with a scroll of paper, saying:

WILL...
YOU...

Now, by now, you'd have thought she'd have known what was coming next, but it is at this point I abandon any pretence at all that she can be considered more intelligent than me, whatever she (or, more often, he) says, because she was genuinely clueless. She defends herself by saying that he had always made it very clear, right from the start, that he would never marry again, having had a short and disastrous previous experience. So she knew where she stood – it was no reflection on her or how he felt about her; it was always known that marriage was never to be on the cards. Ever.

So her surprise was genuine when the final scroll, presented by Digby Dog, said:

MARRY OUR DAD?

Lucky the dogs were there because so high pitched were her squeals of delight that possibly only the dogs could hear them. He whipped out a rather impressive ring and, for the second day in a row, the deal was done... although they didn't seal it by shaking hands...

Most importantly, of course, I approved. Call me old-fashioned, but if I am to live with them, then I would prefer them to be married. To his credit, he seemed to be an admirer of mine, as he was usually pointing a camera at me on the occasions he came to visit me at my hotel or out at a competition, so he is obviously a gentleman of discerning taste. Further in his favour is that he appears to have little interest in making me work. He has sat on my back a few times and wandered about the arena at a walk. He's even managed a few shuffled steps of trot before collapsing into giggles at the bounciness, all of which constitutes the sum total of my desired level of work.

Yes, I approved.

Leaving the Country (Her)

There followed, inevitably, several frustrating months of slow-to-respond solicitors and lenders needing persuading that the property wasn't to be for agricultural use (only in the world of finance can "more than fifteen acres" qualify as agricultural, and this was sixteen acres!) nor for commercial use (her livery yard-running days were long gone). The lenders just didn't seem to take on board that it really was all about me. But, showing the sort of determination and problem-solving that got me into my trailer in the early days, she didn't take "no" for an answer and made it happen, and the lenders found themselves handing over large sums of money with probably much the same startled and bewildered how-did-we-let-that-happen expression on their faces as I bore standing quivering on my trailer about to head off for my first competitions.

And then she left me, abandoned me to fend for myself, in my all-inclusive hotel, while they swanned off to our new home, to fix, tidy and clean it sufficiently for my arrival.

Being a stoic kind of chap and not one to make a fuss, I made the best of it, being ridden by a proper rider in the lovely Freddie, even going out competing with her (successfully, I might add, naturally). But, boy, does she make me work hard ("Properly," she calls it) – usually I "let" my human do most of the work but no such joy with the professional rider on board. My human won't recognise me when she rides me next, I've gone all turbo, from Mondeo to Mercedes in a few schooling sessions. She might want to take Freddie with us, which would be a disaster for my early retirement plan.

So while I was doing all the work, my human was having a lovely, relaxing time packing all their worldly possessions and driving the eleven hours from old home to new.

I am given to understand that it is not entirely normal for buyers to move into their newly purchased property whilst the previous owner still lives there, which makes sense, a bit like me squeezing into my stable while the previous hotel guest is still there – cosy, to say the least. However, their previous owner didn't move out for another six months.

This was by arrangement, I hasten to add, he wasn't an unwanted squatter, but as his own onward house purchase had fallen through they agreed he could stay in one side of the house to allow my humans to get on with their move. His side of the house had its own kitchen and bathroom and staircase and so was entirely independent, having been built as a somewhat generous three-bedroom annex to the original, larger, house. They locked the inter-connecting door and only heard him when Celtic were playing – a football team, I am given to understand, and it is apparently a requirement upon watching your chosen team (the choice of which may or may not be related to your town of birth, and may or may not be related to who won the league in the previous season) run round a field kicking a ball, to shout encouragement or obscenities depending on how the ball-kicking, or opponent-kicking, is going.

Imagine if the shouting thing were the norm for dressage! At least it might drown out the annoying not-quite-German-trained instructor in the warm-up. I rather think I might like being cheered on and having songs and chants made up about me, as long as they didn't start with lines like "who ate all the pies".

On second thoughts, considering the abuse football referees have to put up with, maybe the dressage judges wouldn't welcome a chanting crowd baying for their blood and calling into question their eyesight, or possibly even parentage. I think we consider ourselves above that sort of thing in dressage – by which I mean it is usually reserved for the journey home on bitterly dissecting the marks and comments on our score sheets, accompanied by the sort of language that would make the most hardened of football fans blush. Not really above it at all then. Win or lose, our humans usually partake of a glass or two of a refreshing beverage "post-match" too (pre-match has also been known) – maybe football and dressage aren't so very different after all.

My human's first weeks at the Highlands home were occupied with, quite rightly, addressing immediate issues outside in preparation for my arrival. Prioritising correctly, apart from knocking the worst of the dirt off of their previously uninhabited side of the house, they largely ignored the work needed in there and focussed on my needs.

First on the list was reconfiguring the main stable block from six normal-size stables, some of which were "en-suite" to each other, i.e. with no independent outside door, being accessed via another stable first. Thankfully, my human understood that just because I have no concept of anyone else needing personal space, it doesn't mean that I don't expect a degree of privacy for myself. It simply wouldn't do to have some stranger mooning at me over an internal door between our stables while I am peacefully enjoying my hay net dreaming of sashes, or thinking that he/she can waltz through my own space whenever the need arose. No. So the block was reconfigured into four enormous stables – a vet later was to describe mine as a "suite" in its own right, which is far more acceptable to a gentleman of my standing. My human's thinking was also that if the Highlands winters were as bad as she feared, I may be spending a fair bit of time in my stable, so it wouldn't do me any harm to be able to move about freely in there.

Then they needed to ensure that there was at least one sufficiently and safely fenced field for me, which required a fair bit of time and effort shoring up wobbly posts and removing all sorts of wire, which my human could see getting wrapped round my lovely blemish-free legs and doing their worst.

Finally, they had to address the rabbit holes… hundreds of them, literally, some hidden single-hole leg-breakers, others enormous great warrens which could collapse and swallow a horse whole, and certainly wouldn't leave much of Shorty above-ground. The previous owner was not a horseman but was a nature-lover, so the rabbits had been left unchecked for years to do what rabbits do – multiply and dig. The fields hadn't seen livestock in a while and so were overgrown too, making the humans' job even harder. They resorted to wheel-barrowing tonnes of hardcore around trying to fill in all the holes, at least in my first field to start with, and there discovered the resilience and stubbornness of the Highland bunny – after each day of back-breaking work the humans would return the following morning to find nice, neat, new rabbit holes beside the hardcore-filled ones. However, the bunnies hadn't met my equally stubborn human, whose determination to keep me safe powered her on to keep filling in (or fencing off) holes until she deemed one field safe enough for equine occupation.

And then came the interesting bit – I would need a companion. My human briefly considered getting in a livery, but then remembered all my stress and pacing and shenanigans at previous yards when my fellow field/stable mates went off and did their own thing. She could hardly welcome in a livery and then present them with Yard Rules that basically consisted of "Your horse/pony is to be Bond's shadow at all times", or to be, more crudely, and as the fiancé put it, "Bond's bitch".

This gave her all the excuse she needed to go horse-shopping. Now, while tempted to go and invest in (i.e. risk a vast amount of money on) *another* well-bred dressage youngster, or perhaps a higher-level schoolmaster to show her how to master some more intricate moves (goodness knows she needs all the help she can get), or maybe a solid eventer type so she could have a go at finding her brave pants again, instead she accepted that maybe now wasn't the time to have *two* horses that needed regular proper work and to be aiming at competing two while refurbishing houses and equestrian facilities and finding her way establishing a routine of working from home and being away monthly for work too.

She also had to consider that on those very weeks she would be away, her equine charges would be in the sole care of the fiancé – a chap whose experience of horses was almost entirely encountered from behind a camera. Hugely in his favour, he was, on the whole, unafraid of and unimpressed by the size of us horses, and was willing to get stuck in and do whatever was necessary to help their new lifestyle to work. (This was before he came to learn just how much shovelling was involved – the willingness soon abated, I can tell you, but to his credit he kept on.) However, she couldn't ignore that he had zero experience at such intricacies as the art of putting on headcollars or rugs, or leading to and from fields on windy days when the horse-eating trees might strike and so knew she should aim to find a companion for me that was as user-friendly as possible, to keep all concerned safe. A low-maintenance steed to counter-act the high-maintenance one she already had the pleasure of owning.

There was a part of her that, not entirely secretly, hoped that with the right steed maybe the fiancé would join her on the occasional hack down the beach. She started to form in her mind the ideal second horse for our home – a not too big, not too small, not too quick, not too slow, not too young, not too old, non-reactive, safe but fun, small horse that wouldn't try to kill anyone if it didn't get ridden every day. Actually, according to her, the perfect sort of horse ninety-five per cent of riders should own but don't. A cob then!

If she's completely honest, she would admit she was dreaming of finding a Harry (the super-cob mini-marvel of Jenny's that she had had so much fun eventing) – but maybe not a young Harry, as he had been quite a handful at times in the early days. Maybe a middle-aged Harry – a been there, seen it, done it type. She definitely harboured a hope that she could maybe revisit her glory days of storming round riding club one-day events and venturing outside the dressage arena once again. As long as none of that nonsense involved me, that was fine in my book.

Trouble was, such a paragon of virtue was like gold-dust. And trying to find such a vision of perfection in the sparsely populated, and even more sparsely horsed, Highlands was like trying to find a particular size and stamp of unicorn. On the moon. There was also the fact that such an in-demand little horse would likely be snapped up by a friend of a friend of the seller, long before they had even started to formulate an oh-so-carefully worded advert, and up in Scotland my human didn't yet have any friends, let alone one conveniently selling her ideal second horse.

For a number of weeks literally nothing even remotely suitable appeared in the online adverts that would be within several hours' drive until, finally, she spotted The One. A traditional piebald cob, all mane and feathers, mid-height, mid-age, safe and steady, done a bit of everything but whose young owner now wanted to jump higher and faster and do smarter dressage. Perfect. And only three hours away!

So off they went to try him and were delighted to find he ticked so many boxes. He was really very sweet and easy to do (apart from having his feet picked up – can't wait to tell the farrier). His only other downside was he could be "maybe a little lazy", as his owner said. He certainly made my human work (yes, even more than me!), but she thought, given her dream of riding off into the sunset with her fiancé suitably mounted beside her, that safe and maybe too slow were better than the alternatives. The dream didn't, after all, include his steed spinning, dropping a shoulder, depositing said fiancé in the sea and fluffing off home.

Decision made, the deal was done, and several days later "Elvis", on account of his flared trousers (full-feathered hairy legs), was delivered by his old owners so they could see his new home. He settled straight in, despite being alone (wouldn't catch me putting up with that – hence why she ensured my companion arrived before I did), probably somewhat distracted by the vast amount of grass in the field and the ludicrously large stable. Anyway, he had about three million rabbits to keep him company until I was to make my grand entrance a week or so later.

Elvis was in the building.

Leaving the Country (Me)

Finally, back to me then. Not before time.

My human had lost many a night's sleep (and deservedly so) worrying about how to transport her most precious cargo (me, obviously) the 650 miles from my current luxury hotel in the sunny south to what I was concerned may be some ramshackle old shed surrounded by snow in the deepest darkest north. Other matters also concerned me – would I ever see grass again? Or was it all rocky mountains and snow? Would she have enough rugs for me? Would I understand the strange accents of the Highland ponies? Would they accept a truly softy southerner such as myself? Have they even heard of dressage up there? Or was I supposed to dance around swords while suffering the screeching of bagpipes? Exactly what is haggis? I had so many questions.

Meanwhile, she had (of course) researched my travel options, which didn't take long – either drive me there herself or pay someone else to take me. On the one hand she thought it The Responsible Thing to hand me over to a professional transporter; it's what they *do*, after all. They would have a super-safe vehicle, driver(s) used to such journeys, contacts for appropriate rest points/a stop-over, support if there were problems and I would probably have company in a lorry too.

But, what if I didn't like being in a lorry or my travel companions? What if there was a problem and she wasn't there? Freddie had once said that I would accept doing anything with my little human by my side – this comment prompted after every horse on the yard had had a meltdown on sight of a new land drain across a field gate, dancing up and down it, spinning around and trying to make a run for it, etc. Every horse on the yard, that is, except me, because my human led me to it, stepped over it herself without getting eaten by the drain-monsters that live in it, thereby demonstrating that it was perfectly acceptable for me to do the same. So I did. No drama. I'm not one for making a scene, oh no.

She was, of course, also concerned about driving me for such a distance herself. The journey is a minimum ten hours' driving in a car, plus comfort breaks, so would be at least twelve hours plus breaks towing a trailer, and that's if we managed to avoid any disastrous traffic jams. So we would definitely have to stop half-way for an overnight break for both her and me, and she wasn't sure how I'd cope with both the travelling and settling into a strange stable for a night. She wasn't sure if it was better for her to be there, to help reassure me, or better for her not to see my anxiety that she would be able to do so little about and instead stay at home, try not to think about it, with her metaphorical hands over her ears, repeating la-la-la to pretend it wasn't happening.

But, on balance, she knew in her heart I'd be perfectly happy in my trailer on my own, like normal, versus in a strange lorry with different horses coming and going at various drop-off and pick-up points on the way. So she decided we would take a road trip together like Thelma and Louise, only keeping away from cliffs, hopefully. She checked the route maps, identified a mid-way-ish point as being Carlisle, and found and booked a horse hotel there that took overnight equine guests. When they moved all their worldly goods up there, they left behind at my hotel my trailer and the towing car so my normal mode of transport was all prepared. She just had to fly back down for me!

And, once she had my new home prepared and my companion in place, that's exactly what she did. She packed to the rafters (or she would have done if it had rafters) one side of my trailer with all the bins, crates and boxes that she could fit in, with all *my* worldly goods, plus sufficient hay nets to keep me from starving over the next two days, crammed my tack and her varied collection of saddlery and whatever else she could get into the Jeep, until that too was full to the roof, with only just enough space left for one last critical thing – her co-driver, none other than Sandra, SWMBO, their dog-trainer, landlady, neighbour and all round selfless friend who volunteered to accompany my human on the marathon journey, to co-drive/keep the driver awake/keep the driver calm in the event of any minor issues (because she wouldn't allow major issues).

And so, finally, one Saturday morning, we set off. What an adventure!

My human had been a little concerned that she and SWMBO would struggle for conversation. It was an extremely long time to be in a car with anyone, after all, and, she realised, they had actually never spent any time together on their own – would they have *anything* to talk about?

Turns out, yes, they very much blinking would – from what I could hear from my trailer, anyway. Endless cackling laughter and constant chatter quite disturbed my otherwise serene and calm journey. They stopped off briefly once, when I did get ten minutes' peace, but only after I had recovered from the frankly hysterical, but at the same time embarrassing, sight of the pair of them virtually crawling out of the car and hobbling to the service station. You see, SWMBO was awaiting a partial knee replacement and so was in considerable pain anyway, and my human had been whinging about some problem with her pelvis, so a few hours sat in a car had seized the pair of them up so much they looked twice their age shuffling away. Quite tickled me, if I'm honest. They'd definitely have failed a vetting. In fact, they'd do well to keep away from vets, judging by the state of the pair of them, in case anyone took it upon themselves to "do the kindest thing".

My human had such a fun time with her co-driver that she was perfectly perky enough to continue the drive to our overnight stop-over point in Carlisle. We reached there late afternoon and the kind horse motel managers said I could stretch my legs on the lunge in the school, which was much appreciated. I didn't want to end up looking the same state as the humans, after all, pair of wonky donkeys that they were.

I settled perfectly happily into my motel room, in fact so calmly that my human didn't know whether to be relieved or worried – there really is no pleasing some people. But she could only stay and watch me continuing to placidly munch on my hay net for so long before feeling that she really should get her new BFF to their own hotel and get hay nets of their own.

Unlike my hotel search, which had involved much googling, checking reviews, personal phone calls, etc., their own accommodation was somewhat less well-researched. She had previously used something called Groupon to find the hotels for their property-viewing trip to the Highlands, with great success, staying in some lovely places without having to re-mortgage to do so, and so, believing this method to be fool-proof, used it to book a hotel as close as possible to mine, a few miles away, just in Carlisle city centre.

When they found it, they nearly turned straight around to join me back at my place. If there had been a bit less stuff in the car, they might have kipped in there.

It was grim.

They each had the smallest single bedrooms it can be possible to have. Literally door, bed, window. The car was surely bigger. Their en-suite shower "rooms" were simply claustrophobic enclosures. She hadn't realised that a space in which you could have one foot in the shower and one foot in the loo if you weren't careful could qualify as a "room".

Anyway, they were there now; it was only for one night, so man up and all that (as she is so often heard to say to me). So, on dubiously taking the manager's recommendation for somewhere to get a decent meal within walking distance, they set off down the hotel road towards town, past boarded-up shops, tattoo parlours and suspiciously painted-out windows on premises that still had "open for business" on the door, without specifying exactly what shady business that indeed was. The closer they got to their recommended restaurant, the more the scene was reminiscent of an episode of *Police, Camera, Action* or similar – with police riot vans out, the young, drunk population of Carlisle being variously loudly happy, a bit bloodied or somewhat unwell.

They finally made it to the recommended Italian place and dived inside, fully expecting an indoor version of the scene witnessed outside. How wrong they were! There followed one of the nicest meals she'd had in a long time, possibly assisted by a calming glass of wine or two, plus people-watching to their hearts' content. A fine end to a day far more fun than she had expected!

The following morning dawned and they scarpered out of the hotel without bothering with breakfast on the basis that "facilities" for any resulting emergencies may be few and far between as we ventured off of motorways further north, but, most importantly, made sure I had my last ever "full English". I'd had a very pleasant night and made my human's heart swell with love when I gamely popped back into my trailer as if I had completely forgotten about the previous day's eight-hour marathon journey.

So we set off again, for a far more scenic day's travel. I think the humans were slightly wearier than me, the excitement and hysteria of the previous day somewhat more toned down and my human even allowed her co-driver to actually drive for a couple of hours. And so, many hours later, with huge relief all round, the bumpiness of the track signalled that we had arrived – my new home!

I can't tell you how relieved I was to see that it was not a shack on a snowy mountainside but a real stable, surrounded by grassy fields. Are you sure this is the Highlands of Scotland? It wasn't even raining, let alone snowing.

My own new BFF looked as pleased to see me as I was him. He looked like a kind enough chap, from what I could see under all that hair, although his accent was suspiciously more Irish than Scottish. And while he might beat me in a cuteness competition, he wouldn't hold a candle to me on the catwalk, where it counts, so my ego wasn't threatened either. Yes, he would do just fine.

Highland Home

And so we all settled in to our new home. Elvis was renamed Hamish in a pathetic attempt by my human to make us all a bit more "Highland" (and a bit less Las Vegas). Thankfully she didn't try to rename me Angus or Campbell or MacDougal, or frankly anything pre-fixed with Mac as the fiancé would soon be calling me Big Mac and buying a suspicious amount of burger buns. Particularly worrying given that the nearest fast food establishment is fifty miles away in Inverness and he has always been partial to a Happy Meal or two, having lived off junk food perfectly happily until he met my human. Now she has him eating far more healthily, poor man. I think she was just envious because he lived on a diet of crisps, chocolate, fizzy drinks and takeaway, and still managed to stay perfectly slim and healthy, outwardly at least, while she, like I, is a good-doer and has to be a little more careful to maintain her waistline.

Now Hamish has being a good-doer down to a fine art and all the grass here soon took its toll on his own waistline. My human had to try to restrict his grazing, which was easier said than done given his abject disregard and disdain for the feeble fences. While I, having been brought up to respect anything remotely fence-like (she says, utterly terrified of getting a teeny little electric zap – well, you try it, lady, and we'll see how brave *you* are), wouldn't dream of even approaching so much as a single strand of white rope or tape, unfortunately Hamish's outlook was rather less polite. Basically, if there was a barrier between him and a few more blades of grass, and it was physically possible to flatten or break said barrier, then it was fair game as far as he was concerned. She called him a bulldozer. The fiancé called him other things.

It was at this point that The Fencing Programme commenced – a vast, and vastly expensive, plan to post and rail fence all the fields. This had always been the plan, to have neat and tidy beautifully fenced paddocks, but Hamish's activities somewhat accelerated it up the list of Urgent Things to Do, leap-frogging such luxuries as ridding the human's lounge of damp, installing a cooker and replacing the boiler.

Phase One was the immediate and urgent installation of a Hamish-proof fence around just one of the fields, ideally the one with least grass in. Poor Hamish was going to get the same treatment as the fiancé, cutting down all his favourite things to eat.

The humans' imagination in naming each of the fields for easy identification and discussion purposes knew no bounds. "Beach Field" ran beside the beach,

"School Field" was beside the school, "Big Field" – you'll never guess – was the biggest field, and so it went on. A tiny bit of imagination went into naming the last two: "Golf Field", in which he was known to chip a ball or two with his bats, reminiscing about days gone by when he had time and energy for such a hobby, and "Watership Down" – by far the worst rabbit warren-scarred area, from which us horses were to be banned for literally years for our own safety.

And so School Field was the chosen land for Hamish's dietary doom. An extraordinary amount of money was spent extraordinarily quickly and before he knew it Hamish had a super-smart, super-empty field to remain healthy in, while I rather smugly stuffed my face with lots of lovely grass in the barely fenced fields beside him.

I was very happy in my new home from Day One. Hamish was a good companion, safe and unruffled and stoic. We were turned out and brought in at the same time without fail, and no other horses came or went, so my anxiety all but disappeared. I was calm and relaxed and very easy to manage and all boded well for the fiancé being left to take care of Hamish and I whenever my human had to work down south (or "down the road", as they say up here).

There were only two triggers that would make me have to remind my human just who she had brought home. The first was on the occasions when she rode Hamish out. I allowed her to ride him in the arena without taking issue, but woe betide her if she rode him towards the gate down to the beach. I would (and still do) neigh and neigh and neigh, apparently hysterically, and non-stop until the moment they arrive back home.

The first time she did it she expected, from the amount of "ludicrous screaming" she heard from the beach, to arrive back to find me in a terrible state, head to toe white lather, having torn round and round my stable. But no, I'm not quite the "moron" I have been, in my view totally unnecessarily, labelled. When she arrived back from deserting me for twenty long minutes, I was unmarked, hadn't even broken sweat, barely moved. The fiancé had, unbeknown to me, been spying on me and had witnessed that I had been perfectly calmly standing at my door simply yelling my anger at being left behind. I still do it to this day, despite being in the full knowledge that my companion and human will return in a short while like they always do. The fiancé absolutely hates it. It amuses me.

The other trigger for any angst is when I have to demonstrate to my human that it is time to bring us horses in from our fields. This may be because it is windy. Or raining. Or cold. Or late. Or a day with a y in it. Or I don't like the way that seagull is looking at me. I don't need a reason; it's just *time*. So then I fence-pace, just like the old days! Frustratingly, that doesn't get an immediate reaction. Clearly, no longer being at a horse hotel means that the service is slow and, at times, frankly rubbish. I'm sure I've seen her at her window watching me, rolling her eyes and then not appearing for another hour. She says she's not having me train her into leaping to my side every time I decide I want something. I can't believe her attitude. Appalling. Doesn't she know who I am? She'll never get five stars at this rate.

It doesn't help my cause that because we are right beside the beach, our fields have extremely sandy free-draining soil, absolutely not the bottomless clay I'm used to. So while my occasional fence-pacing efforts may wear a track of sorts, the grass soon grows over it, and it isn't a foot deep requiring filling in with hardcore, lime and topsoil, as "may" have happened elsewhere. I am no longer a mud-making machine, we don't have mud!

Something my human had been anxious about (see, it's not just me) was just how much professional equine support would be available so far north. Would the vets be more used to treating Highland cows? Would she have to take a crash course in hoof trimming? Would she have to import quality hay, feed and bedding? When she asked about a horse physio, would she be locked away for talking like a mad woman?

Turns out I'm not the only one that needn't have worried. Her neighbouring friendly farmer supplied her with straw and, initially, hay too but in subsequent years made hay for her off her own fields, and there was a horse feed shop not two miles away, which would order in whatever my heart desired.

She found a truly lovely farrier, Barrie, that I approved of enormously because he talked daft to me and let me rest my head on his back when he did my front feet, and let me rest my back feet on him when he did those. He was also a bit of a magician when it came to the reluctant-to-comply Hamish. Hamish was barefoot and only needed a trim, so you'd think he could tolerate a farrier's attention for ten minutes. But no. He had farriers hanging off his wildly waving legs; he snatched his feet away and slammed them back to the floor so hard the ground shook; steel toe-caps were compulsory footwear round him at farrier o'clock; he'd spin about, try to flatten the poor chaps against the wall – he was really rather brutish about the whole thing.

And then Barrie would stroll over, talk more daft to the shifty-looking Hamish, pick up a leg and, usually after a trial waggle, Hamish would go all limp and surrender as quickly and entirely as my human does her willpower on sight of a box of Lindt chocolates, i.e. a split second of token hesitation, followed by, "Oh, go on then."

Fortuitously, as it turns out, there was also a highly regarded purely equine veterinary practice near Inverness. And even a horse physio just a few miles away. All my needs were covered. It was going to be alright.

Eventually.

Surgery?!

It was at one such physio treatment that the lovely lady who normally makes my back feel better said that it looked like I was probably ready for my annual kissing spine injection. Expecting as much and not concerned, my human made the arrangement with the vets who then came out and did the same procedure as had been undertaken for a number of years now. So far, so normal.

Trouble was, my back still hurt.

My human wasn't sure – the injection had always worked fabulously, why should this time be any different? Had I, coincidentally, tweaked my back or pelvis somehow after the injection, masking its beneficial effects with another type of back pain? The physio returned but considered that my pain was exactly as it had been pre-injection; it was as if it hadn't happened at all.

More concerned now, my human booked me in for a trip to the vet's clinic for further investigation. The vet practice made my appointment to coincide with a day when their consulting surgeon from the Edinburgh Vet

School would be in attendance, so I could see the very best. There, they X-rayed my back and it was confirmed that the kissing spine had worsened and so the steroid injections could no longer be considered enough to manage it. The surgeon suggested, though, that the nature of my spine damage, still being relatively mild compared to the likes of the ill-fated Gem, made me an ideal candidate for surgery.

A wave of horror swept over my human at the prospect. She had researched kissing spine surgery years ago for Gem and, at that time, it largely involved quite a brutal procedure whereby, under general anaesthetic, sections of the spinous processes were completely removed through a large incision. It was a hugely invasive and traumatic surgery, from which the recovery was lengthy and extensive, including months of box rest and recuperation and rehabilitation. And it didn't guarantee success.

Fortunately, the surgeon had spotted the colour drain from my human's face as soon as he mentioned the word surgery and realised she must be thinking of the full-on removal of pieces of spine version. He quickly advised her of the relatively new procedure he was thinking would be more appropriate in my case – whereby, under a standing sedation and local anaesthetic, they "simply" snip the ligaments (thought to be the source of the pain associated with kissing spine) that are present between each spinous process through keyhole incisions as guided by the X-rays.

While naturally still enormously concerned, my human was comfortable that this option gave me the best possible chance of a longer and more active life. Personally I wouldn't have minded the retirement option the vet also mentioned, as my back pain is only experienced when ridden... but apparently "we" aren't at that stage yet... and so the appointment was made for the surgeon's next visit date.

She then went home and did what every right-minded, sensible, intelligent, informed, experienced individual would do – she googled "kissing spine ligament snip surgery" and read about every horror story, every failed attempt, every infected wound, every lost horse until she'd thoroughly wound herself up that I was, in fact, doomed, and it was all her fault for agreeing to it.

And so, one long and largely sleepless month (for her, while for me one not-long-enough holiday) later, I made the trip back to the vet clinic for the surgeon to perform the procedure. To my human's pleasant surprise, it was to be, if all went well, a day case and she would be able to bring me home later in the afternoon after I recovered from the sedation. Which was a relief for her for many reasons, not least of which was that we were forecast our first taste of Highland snow the next day and she didn't fancy towing me about in my trailer in those conditions, in whatever state I might be in.

We arrived at the clinic and she saw me safely to my day stable. The surgeon spoke to her briefly to confirm the procedure and how the day was expected to unfold, then she was left with the vet nurse to discuss details and when she should return to collect me.

She was just about to tear herself away from me when, in a moment of madness, she thought to ask if it would be possible for her to stay and watch. The vet nurse was just starting on the long list of reasons why they don't allow that sort of thing (not ideal to have vomiting owners, crying owners, owners asking the surgeon hundreds of questions, owners quoting HappyHacker267 off of some forum who said the surgeon should do something a certain way, etc., etc.) when said surgeon happened to breeze past, overhearing my human's request, and just said, "I don't see why not," which rather stopped the poor vet nurse in her tracks and, given the near-reverential way the clinic staff spoke to and of the surgeon, she immediately had to back-track and allow my somewhat equally surprised human in.

She's a funny old thing, that Shorty. By her own admission she would confess that she could be a bit squeamish at times and, despite her loving nothing more than a film or TV drama, or indeed book, with a good few deaths in it, when it comes to it, she may find a sudden interest in watching the dogs sleeping on the sofa opposite when it all gets a bit too gory and real on screen.

So you'd think the prospect of seeing her beloved noble steed approached by a surgeon and commencing a scene reminiscent of an episode of *Silent Witness*, one of her favourites (for dog-watching), that she'd run a mile. But, understandably, she loves the very bones of me (while not enjoying the prospect of actually seeing them) and can't bear the thought of leaving me to go through something this important without her.

So there we were – me standing in some sort of stocks arrangement, blissfully unaware, sedated off into the Olympics, where I was pirouetting and piaffing my way through winning the freestyle to my musical score, which sounded suspiciously like the theme tune to *Casualty*, while she stands nervously (whilst trying to look calm and relaxed in case she gets removed) at my head which, incidentally, is resting on a huge, padded crutch-like affair to allow me to be as dozy as possible whilst still remaining upright. I approved, might like one for my stable actually.

And so it started. She knew she was going to have a tough job without any sleeping dogs to watch when the surgeon, having made his first keyhole incision and done some initial ferreting about, picked up two instruments which looked suspiciously to her like a hammer and chisel. This simple ligament "snip" was looking less like a little light *Kirsty's Homemade Christmas* and a little more *DIY SOS*. However, to her credit, she remained upright and focussed, and even when one of the vet nurses, at a particularly yukky bit, asked if she was OK, she still managed a wry smile, an eye roll and some comment about having probably gone off the idea of popping out to a carvery for her lunch.

Afterwards she said that actually she was genuinely glad she'd seen the true nature of the procedure, as it gave her a better understanding of, and appreciation for, the recovery and rehab I'd need.

The surgeon was happy with his work and I'd won the all-important sash in my Olympic dream, so my human took me safely home later that day.

Good job she did, as the next day we all woke to three feet of snow! Timed to perfection, as I was on two weeks' box rest anyway, so she only needed to dig her way to my door sufficiently to muck me out and keep my water and hay topped up. I think Hamish was almost as relieved as I that he wasn't expected to go and stand out in the snow, with him being on Companion Duty and sharing my box rest fate, quite contentedly.

Home Sweet Home

The snow finally thawed just in time for my walking in hand exercise to begin and then, shortly after, to allow Hamish and me to be safely turned out during the day again.

My human followed the vets' instructions carefully, and I had several physio sessions too to ensure everything recovered just as it should. Eventually it was time for my human to saddle and mount me once more. She was so tentative about the process, it was almost comical. There was a part of her that was terrified I would snap in two the moment her bottom touched down on the saddle (I noticed that wasn't incentive enough for her to maybe shift a few pounds as the day was looming, though, but hey ho, not *that* terrified then), but of course I was absolutely fine. She knew in her heart I would be because of the way the rest of my recovery had gone – the physio was delighted with me, I was moving freely and soundly when we had done our light lunging, and, a ground-breaking discovery for both of us, I had stopped dipping away from the passing of a brush over my back whenever she groomed me. Apparently, I had always done it and she had thought it was just because I'm a sensitive soul (*moi?*), but now she can give me a sound grooming and my back no longer automatically reacts as if she's using a wire brush to beat me with, bouncing up and down like the orange space hopper that I am.

It was especially during this time that she and I were so very grateful for our incredible hacking. The endless sandy beach is literally on our doorstep and gave me the ideal consistent supportive but giving surface to regain my strength and fitness without risking damaging my legs or, what she was particularly worried about, stumbling on uneven ground and tweaking my back while it was still weak.

And neither of us miss the roadwork! I'm pretty robust around traffic, to be fair, but the lanes around a couple of my former hotels were often busy with impatient whizzy cars and vans which my human hated even more than I did. My one horror that we encountered occasionally near Freddie's hotel was the like of which I had never seen before. As was to become the norm, the first time we came across it I heard it before I saw it – a thundering, clanking, jangling cacophony of noise, the source of which was unseen, advancing quickly towards us around a bend in the high-hedged single track road. Rarely for me, I was genuinely scared.

And then I saw it.

And then I was genuinely terrified.

Four enormous horses, all kind of tied together, advancing at a spanking great trot which was faster than my finest medium canter, being very closely chased by some odd engineless roofless car arrangement (a carriage, so my human explained later). They hammered towards me, bearing down on us in a lane no wider than the alleged "carriage", so I did the only intelligent sensible thing.

I scarpered.

Turned tail and ran for home, my human frantically trying to pull me up, at least by enough to stop me skidding over on the slippery tarmac, but not by too much and so allow the horses and carriage to shorten the distance between us again. Their driver either didn't know or didn't care about the effect he was having on us, as he just kept coming. And so, as it turned out, he would continue to do so each time he encountered either me or any of the other horses at my hotel. All the humans were not entirely complimentary about him. We were known to dive up farm tracks and even people's driveways on sight or sound of him. My human learnt to accept my signal that I had heard them before her (neck bolt upright and rigid, ears meeting in the middle, with a sudden desperate urge to spin round) and would happily agree with my suggestion – let's *go*. We developed quite the spanking trot of our own and limited the amount of times we would see the Carriage of Carnage again.

Nothing so terrifying on our beach. In fact, there's nothing on our beach at all, usually. We rarely see anyone on our travels – the occasional dog and human, even less occasionally a horse and human from the farm up the lane. But usually it's all ours, just the way we like it. I don't even mind cantering through the water, as it's so very shallow as the land there is so flat, and the water is clear so I can tell that there are no sharks or sea monsters lurking. And not a flying horse-eating monster insect in sight. It's pretty perfect, really.

A handful of times the fiancé did join us on Hamish, who was exceptionally well behaved (i.e. slow). He even mastered rising trot, which he couldn't on me due to my obscenely bouncy trot. Even at a jog my human struggles with sitting trot on me, and the very few riders she has allowed on me over the years have all exclaimed over how I seem to fire them out of the saddle with every stride. What can I say? I'm just such a powerhouse. Hamish, however, just kind of mooches along, perhaps his fatty pads providing more comfort for his rider (I can be such a bitch sometimes).

But even with his armchair steed, the fiancé just didn't take to riding, didn't see the joy of it at all, even on that amazing beach. He said he'd rather be walking the dogs along it. I have to admit that at the crux of it is the point that, even with my obvious charms and attractions, he just doesn't love us horses anything like my human does and so there is no attraction to him for spending time with us.

I rather think poo has a lot to do with it. Mine and Hamish's, to be clear. He seems to think that there's rather a lot of it. He's used a couple of handfuls (in bags, I hasten to add) of dog poop a day, not a couple of wheelbarrows full.

Whereas my human simply *loves* to pick up after us. She obviously can barely wait to get started every day. She gives us breakfast in our stables and immediately starts mucking out while I leisurely munch nice and slowly until I've licked the bowl clean while she gets to do the jobs she loves before she has to be at her desk by 8am. She enjoys it so much that then in the afternoons, after work, she comes out to the field with a shovel and wheelbarrow to do it all again.

Well, she did, until he bought her a quad bike and poo vac, and now she has to slum it just riding around pointing an overgrown Henry Hoover and zapping all of my and Hamish's hard work. I'm sure she prefers the old way; she always used to talk to herself while doing it. Well, more muttering, really, accompanied by a certain look in the direction of us happily grazing equines. Probably thanking us for giving her the chance to be out in the fresh air (rain) and saving her the fortune she'd otherwise have to spend going to a gym to get the same level of weight-lifting exercise. Every day. Now she just jaunts about on that quad bike wearing what must be a completely fake grin, saying strange things like, "Game-changer," and, "This is what it must have been like when they first invented washing machines." Poor thing.

Whereas the fiancé says that the work-to-pleasure ratio of having horses is all wrong. Bizarrely, he can't see that the fortunes spent buying and keeping us and the time and effort spent looking after us doesn't make a few rides a week (if it's not raining) worth it. Well, he would think that; he doesn't even like riding.

But to his credit, when she goes back "down the road" for work each month, he does take care of us: mucking out, bringing in and out, feeding, haying, etc. He doesn't like it, but he does it.

Meanwhile she has to endure several days without such pleasures. She quickly got used to flying regularly, following a self-imposed psychological kick up the derriere. Having never flown alone she was overwhelmed the first time, despite little Inverness Airport being probably one of the least intimidating airports in the world. There were tears on the first take-off (embarrassing for her when she's with someone, embarrassing for everyone else when she isn't), but she reminded herself that this was "part of the deal" and told herself to get over it in much the same way as she has been heard to say to me… many, many times. Good to know she practises what she preaches once in a while.

Another of her fears was, on the homeward bound trip, not finding her way around Gatwick, fearing missing her flight and roaming the miles of corridors in the wrong terminal for days before security found her and interrogated her, not believing her tale that someone of her age and intelligence could be so stupid as to not be able to catch a plane on their own.

But she was soon sweeping through Gatwick with the same bored nonchalance as a commuter through London Victoria, looking with barely disguised annoyed disdain at the over-excited holiday-makers, so easily identified by their outfits – either "beach-ready" at Gatwick in January, or, having carefully read health and safety advice for recommended travel attire, in their most "comfortable" (ugly) loose trousers and shoes to slip off while crammed into their teeny tiny allocated space, complete with neck pillow, bottle of water and books, all for their forty-minute flight to Paris.

Her time while down south was spent rather like a student cramming for exams, only with less poverty and vomiting. She worked long days in the office and then spent most evenings out seeing friends and family. She had been extraordinarily lucky enough to be offered the use of a spare room at Freddie's, which was a self-contained space with kitchenette and bathroom, so she could come and go without disturbing anyone and have a dinner-go-ping on the rare evenings she wasn't out wining and dining. So she still regularly saw all the people she had feared she would miss by moving so far away. She really felt like she had the best of both worlds.

Alongside Freddie's family's generosity in letting her stay, SWMBO and her husband Richard also continued to demonstrate their kindness by letting her keep her little Mini Cooper at theirs so she had her own transport down south too (and it meant she still got to see them and those four German Shepherds every visit without fail). That is, until the day her flight home was cancelled.

It had been a sweltering hot few days and my human was so looking forward to getting home to a more pleasant heat and a beach breeze. She had barely been able to sleep it was so hot in the room in the barn roof at Freddie's, so for once she really couldn't wait for her evening flight, back to her cool stone cottage and a decent night's sleep. And to see her beloved steed, of course!

She boarded her flight as normal and they were all ready to go. Then, to the dismay of all the passengers, the pilot warned them that there was to be not only a delay but also a risk that the flight may be cancelled completely. Apparently, there were storms causing havoc on their route north which meant they couldn't take off yet, and if they waited too long then Inverness Airport would close, as it did at 10pm, so they wouldn't be able to take off at all.

This news triggered the apparently rarest of events – it meant complete strangers sitting next to each other on the plane actually talked to each other to share their moans and groans. Turns out my human's seat-buddy lived in the next town north of her (i.e. pretty close neighbours by Highlands standards) and he too had been down south on business. They waited, making vague awkward small talk under the Emergency Protocol for Strangers guidelines (jobs, weather), until the pilot made the fateful apologetic announcement that due to circumstances beyond their control... blah blah. Everybody off.

All the disgruntled passengers were herded like sheep through passport control (bizarrely, given that they hadn't actually been anywhere) and were then guided to the airline's help desk to rebook their flights. It was hot and chaotic, too many grumpy people pushing and shoving – no stoic Brits waiting patiently in line here. My human, somewhere towards the back of a throng of hundreds of people and items of baggage, at least had the foresight to see if she could book a flight online but found that there were no empty seats for the next couple of days and the first ones after that were horribly expensive. She even looked online at sleeper train availability, but it was the middle of the summer holidays and there was nothing. She just wanted to be out of this heat and home! Her horses needed her!

She phoned the fiancé to update him and they were discussing the options – returning to the room to sweat it out for a few days until she could get home, or the possibility of her finding a flight from Heathrow, maybe, to Aberdeen or even Glasgow, and him driving for several hours to collect her from that airport. She knew she couldn't drive the whole way home herself; it was already 10pm and she was shattered after a sleep-deprived week, and even if she tried to drive half-way there was no guarantee of finding somewhere to sleep to break up the exhausting journey, with it being the school holidays.

And then she spotted her seat-buddy also loitering about uncertainly, and in a split second she formulated the kind of random plan only she would conjure up. The kind of thinking that got us living in the Highlands in the first place. Random. Not normal.

While still on the phone to the fiancé, she virtually pounced on the poor unsuspecting seat-buddy and in a breathless rush said that she had a car here; would he share the drive back home with her? She was proposing that they basically spend the night in a car together and she didn't even know his name!

Now she isn't (contrary to evidence) completely naïve or bonkers, and in that split second she did consider that he might be a crazed serial killer and that she was just offering him on a plate his next victim, but she also felt like sometimes you just have to go with your instinct and trust that the world is generally full of mostly quite nice people. Who just want to go home.

To the man's credit he didn't turn and run away from what was clearly a crazy woman. He did a lot of really rather un-serial-killer-like things such as phoning his wife and taking my human's and the Mini's details to add to his insurance cover for twenty-four hours.

Then they jumped in a cab to SWMBO's to collect the Mini, filled her up (the Mini, not SWMBO) and, at 11pm, started their long journey.

With a sense of déjà-vu, my human wondered what on earth they could find to talk about, two complete strangers, to keep whoever was driving awake. Turned out, once again, quite a lot actually. They learnt that they were similar ages, had both been born and raised in Essex, so knew all the same dodgy pubs and nightclubs, both moved to Surrey/West Sussex in their first marriages, where both marriages ended (nothing against Surrey/West Sussex, I'm sure), both even lived in the same village at one point! His second wife was an accountant, and they had lived in the Highlands for a few years longer, but, best of all, they had horses for years too!

Now while she was sharing her life history and answering such searching and intimate questions as,

"Duran Duran or Spandau Ballet?" and, "U2 or Bon Jovi?", the fiancé and I were both fence-pacing (literally), only slightly reassured by her texted updates throughout the night whenever she wasn't driving. There was serious concern, on both side of the fence, that I would be left with the fiancé to look after me indefinitely and, although he does everything that is needed, frankly, I prefer my breakfast served with kisses and, "Good morning, gorgeous," and my rugs changed with scratches and admiring words, all of which are somewhat lacking in his attentions to my needs.

I think it's safe to say we all had a pretty sleepless night, so imagine the relief all round when finally, at 10am, she pulled that amazing little car safely into the driveway and flopped, rather wobbly, into the arms of her human. There were tears, I can tell you. Not mine, obviously, I just wandered nonchalantly off grazing. Me? Bovvered? Whatever.

And so, apart from the odd excitement such as this, life settled into a pleasant and contented routine. I was gradually ridden more and the work stepped up until I was signed off by the professionals as fit and healthy and probably stronger than I'd ever been.

Hamish got off far more lightly. His job description had pretty much become almost entirely "Companion", having been made redundant from his position as "Plod for Novice" and considered unsuitable for the role of "Riding Club Eventer". He occasionally got taken for a stroll along the beach by my human, but I don't think either of them were bothered about doing it too often.

And then, out of the blue, Hamish's old owner got in contact and asked if there was any way my human would sell him back to her. Her new horse, his replacement, a young Irish mare, had been a bit of a disaster with episodes of lameness and colic, plus had made a significant dent in the poor girl's confidence (as well as bank balance) with the mare's ridden antics – she just wanted her lovely old boy back. My human could see that Hamish was being wasted with us and that pretty much any gelding could be my companion, whereas only one boy could make that young lady happy again. And so she agreed. All she asked was that she was given time to find a replacement so I wasn't left alone – as that most certainly would *not* go down well.

And so, once again, her search began.

How Not to
Buy a Horse

Having eliminated from her list of requirements the need for Companion#2 to be ploddy enough to be safe for the fiancé to ride, she could consider something a bit more fun for herself, while still needing to be safe and easy to handle and manage – a sports cob then!

However, once again, the remoteness of our geographical location really limited the potential market and she struggled to find anything suitable within a few hours' radius. For a while she thought she'd found a cracker but then the seller changed her mind about selling. She even considered trying horses when she was next down south and having one transported up here if she found the right one.

She was aware that time was ticking on and Hamish's old/new owner really wanted him as soon as possible. At this point she stumbled across a post on Facebook by the lady at whose PRE stud I had stayed at briefly. The post related to several horses for sale, conveniently, if bizarrely, in Scotland, one of which was a rather lovely-looking PRE gelding.

My human contacted the Scottish seller with a number of questions and got a short and simple reply. Due to a sudden family bereavement several horses were for sale but there were to be no conversations, no hundreds of questions, no trying the horse, no vetting. The family just couldn't deal with it all. Basically, if you like the look of one of the horses and want it, come and get it. It was cheap.

Now, over the years, my human has been asked numerous times by friends and clients, her opinion on horse-buying. She has attended viewings for and with several people, and offered advice on suitability and potential. Not once, on any of those occasions, did that advice include, "Yeah, go on, just go and pay for and collect a horse you've only seen a photo of, not met or ridden it, not been able to ask any questions about its history, soundness, quirks, vices, management issues, temperament, etc., etc."

But that's exactly what she did.

She can't explain why, but she just felt like it was one of those "meant to be" things, and so, ignoring common sense and everything she had learnt over the years, just a few days later she hitched up my trusty trailer and drove the three hours to collect my new companion. While there, she did manage to have a long chat with his seller, the poor girl whose father had sadly died in an awful accident on the farm, and got lots of information on the horse, and then she brought him home.

A bit like the horses and carriage, I heard him before I saw him. He arrived doing what he had apparently been doing for the last three hours – clattering around the trailer and yelling his head off (and she says I make a fuss when I'm left alone! At least I travel sensibly) while my human had spent three hours wondering just what on earth had she done, what sort of crazed lunatic horse she had been mug enough to buy.

However, he settled well enough in the field next to mine and only the very next day Hamish was collected to return to the loving arms of his previous home.

Then I got to meet the new chap properly and learn more about him. I have to admit he's rather a good-looking little fellow. As a pale dapple grey with dark mane and tail, he looks like a rocking horse. He's 15.2hh, so I still get to look down on him, physically as well as psychologically, and a youngster at just eight years old, so I can give him the benefit of my wisdom, if he'll stand still long enough to listen.

He was bred in Spain, a purebred Andalusian (PRE) and imported as a young stallion at two years old, to my human's old stomping ground, Essex. As a result, he has quite an odd accent – a bit *The Only Way is Malaga*, and he has a penchant for diamante browbands. Which is something we have in common.

As a three-year-old they tried to back him but found him too much of a handful and, after he reportedly "fell out" with his owner's trainer, he found his way to the Scottish farm as a four-year-old. There he promptly ran through fences and was generally a bit of a hooligan, so the inevitable happened – off with his bits! A stunning well-bred stallion is all very well, but if he's unrideable and unmanageable then no one wants to breed from him and he's just a dangerous, destructive field ornament.

Thankfully, as a gelding, he became a delightful young man. He's cheeky and comical still, but in a harmless, appealing way. On arrival at my home, he did try being a bit bossy with me in the field, but, much to my human's amazement, I didn't rise to it and challenge him, I let it wash over me and allowed him to guide me round the field, lulling him into thinking I was a docile old boy and he was Alpha.

Which I was, and he was, until early winter when my human starts putting hay in the field to supplement the grazing during the day as an incentive to stop me from fence-pacing to demonstrate my desire to be brought back into the stable within thirty minutes of being turned out in the morning. I do *not* share my hay; I *do* choose which hay net I want to eat from in the field; that *may* change every five minutes. And just one death-ray glare from my direction to BB's (posh name Habanero BBB) conveyed that without any need for biting or kicking or any such dramatic handbags at dawn. And so, just like that, it was established that in fact I was Alpha, and he was my little friend.

Bless him, he tried the Alpha thing with our human at first too. I could have told him he'd get short shrift there and I was right; she was having none of it. But again, as he is such a sensitive little soul, it also takes little more than a death-ray glare from her, or at most a sharp, "*Oy,*" and he was back in line again. She soon found him to be really rather affectionate and cuddly, and he'll stand all day making funny faces when she scratches or grooms him.

And she loves riding him! We are very different, totally opposite ends of the spectrum, which she enjoys as it challenges her. I am more serene, calm, steady, wise and knowledgeable (she, rather uncharitably, calls it lazy and clever, and not necessarily clever in a good way), while he is all young, agile and eager.

And clueless.

He hadn't been in much work when she got him and had largely just hacked since he was finally gelded and backed. So he was a blank canvas in the school, but super-sensitive, very forward-going, if wobbly, and desperate to please and learn.

As I say, we are very different.

There was a time I would have been very unhappy about sharing my human to such an extent, but I can see its benefits now. The more work he does, the less I have to do. Often she will school him and then turn to me and say, "How about a stroll on the beach?" Sounds good to me. And that's on the days when she rides us both – more often we take it in turns each day – result!

Preparation for the Big Day

Further saving me from over-work, she has also been occupied with renovating the houses, once the previous owner finally moved out.

With the intention of ending up with a holiday cottage, they entirely redecorated "his" side and added another shower room, fully furnished it and then moved into it themselves in order to do the more major works to their side of the house. This took many, many months as the humans discovered the "Highland Way", a philosophy of the trades much like the Spanish "Manyana", which basically meant that all builders, plumbers, electricians, carpenters, plasterers and the like were as elusive as a 10 in a dressage test.

Incidentally, the first time she got such a coveted and rare score was on Rubbish, at his first competition back after recovering from damaging a suspensory ligament. They had completed the test and returned to the trailer, and she was just untacking him when a car approached and the driver called out to her, "Were you the last rider in that class I was just judging?" and my human, immediately terrified that the judge had spotted some degree of lameness that she wasn't aware of, gave a feeble, worried little, "Yeeeeess," at which point the judge said, "I just wanted to thank you for such a lovely test, and that last centre line I simply couldn't fault so I gave you my first-ever 10." They had won! Needless to say, of course, my human cried and hugged dear Rubbish, some things don't change.

Anyway, the elusiveness of the Lesser Spotted Highland Plumber and his pals only started to cause anxiety as the months approaching The Big Day drew near. Not one for making life easy for herself, it had been decided that they wanted to be married here at home, as it is legal to do in Scotland. The plan was to have a marquee in beach field, with a view out over the beach and firth and the mountains on the other side of the water, with us horses looking on. All very romantic.

As long as it wasn't blowing a gale.

Plan B was decorating the barn opposite the stables – we would still be looking on!

After the ceremony, they would then take themselves off to a local castle hotel for their feeds and human dressage to music.

However, this grand plan meant that as much as possible in the houses (where family would stay) and outside (where every guest would see) needed to be as spick and span as possible, rather quicker than would otherwise be necessary.

The humans had already completed a huge amount of work outside, largely taking down and getting rid of run-down old buildings, like a big dilapidated goat barn that had sat just a few paces from their back door, totally blocking the view from the house out to the fields, complete with waist-deep ancient goat bedding (the bedding was ancient; I have no idea how old the last resident goats had been).

There had also been lean-to additions to the main ancient old stone barn steading, which they removed to restore it to its original form. Plus various kennels, aviaries, greenhouses and sheds, all somewhat past their prime.

The stables, meanwhile, though in a modern, purpose-built block and while they had been reconfigured inside in the first few weeks, still had the old fronts on them which were half-height chipboard and the rest heavy-gauge cable mesh, which made it look rather like a cheap horse jail. Plus when the wind blew the snow around, it came through the bars of the jail and settled inside the stables, somewhat defeating the object of trying to keep us poor beasts away from the elements.

The one trade person who regularly not only agreed to come out to quote, but *actually* quoted, *and* even returned to do the work as commissioned, was the fencing chap. In the months leading up to the wedding, his services were in high demand, not only fencing other fields but also replacing the jail cell facades with some really rather smart (and weather-proof) timber stable doors and walls. I approved – much more befitting a gentleman of my breeding.

The other area that I considered needed attention was my all-important arena. When I arrived, it was an overgrown oval-shaped patch of grassy, weedy sand, which, many, many years ago, had some rubber chips put on top. Surrounding it, rather oddly, were hundreds of tyres, acting as banks or as a fence of sorts, but really only serving to make it look like a BMX track or breaker's yard. It needed more than a few flowerpots and a mirror to make it look like a dressage arena, I can tell you.

Thankfully, the humans agreed and set about tearing out and disposing of the hundreds of tyres and then, to my utter joy, got a digger in and had it extended to a real life 60m x 20m arena of my very own. More rubber chip was delivered and spread, and the fencing man did his fencing thing and then, there it was: the super-smart full-size dressage arena of my dreams. I was one happy bunny. My human was pretty chuffed too. There would be no stopping us now!

They also painted everywhere too – not just decorating the entire inside of their renovated house, but also the stone barn steading and the stable block too. Basically, if it didn't move, it got painted. In fact, a few things that *did* move still got painted, so feverish were their labours, mainly the dogs' tails and one of the chickens I recall trying out a new look with white highlights in her copper feathers.

The three chickens had come with the property. They were ladies of advancing years even when we arrived, well past their egg-laying days, but my humans didn't have the heart to get the previous owner to rehome them (or worse), and so for far more years than anyone expected, they occupied one of the barns by night and were free range by day, hence the redecoration of the friendliest of them.

In fact, she wasn't just friendly, she was downright nosy (beaky?) and, in particular, would follow my human about all over the place to the extent she called her their third German Shepherd. Sometimes her recall was better than the genuine German Shepherds too. She often found her way into my stable and many's the time I ended up sharing my feed with her, cheeky chook. She had free access to my stable, as opposed to the others because, until my door was finally closed for the night, there was merely a chain across the doorway, which, being the sensible grown-up that I am, I respected and stayed behind without question. Unlike Hamish, who, in his quest for a blade of grass outside, inevitably barrelled through his, taking a chunk of doorway with him, and BB, who limboed under his, just because he could. Honestly, kids these days, no respect.

As The Big Day approached my human became more and more nervous. Not, as you'd expect, about fluffing her lines or tripping over her dress, but about injuring herself in advance and finding herself not so much carried over the threshold once married, but carried to the ceremony on account of spraining her ankle falling off a ladder, or dropping off of one of her fine horses (through no fault of their own) or some other stupid act of clumsiness.

She is rather accident-prone. And she often manages it all by herself with no intervention from others, not even me. In recent months she had managed to crack a rib while painting some bannisters. And not, as you'd imagine, falling off a ladder or down the stairs – oh no, she doesn't always need such obvious props to assist her in her unintentional self-harming. This time she was, really rather incredibly stupidly, leaning over a bannister at the top of the stairs and – just stretching to reach that last bit – took her feet off the ground, risking tumbling head first into the stair well, and as she was wriggling about to stretch, with all her weight on the bannister across her middle, she heard it snap. Not the bannister. Her rib. Literally, heard it go "crump", followed by the inevitable excruciating pain.

She knew what she'd done immediately, having broken ribs before. At least the first time she had some assistance, from dear Rubbish, who crushed her between himself and the stable door once in his keenness to be turned out, naughty boy – and she says I have no spatial awareness! At least that time she went to hospital (by ambulance, who had to scrape her off the floor where she was on her knees in agony).

This time she finished her painting (yes, really) and didn't even let on to the fiancé what she had done (it was the day before her birthday so didn't want to spoil the day!), compounding her utter stupidity, presumably in the hope that if she pretended it hadn't happened then it would magically go away. Funnily enough, that didn't happen, and I had a delightful couple of weeks' holiday while she was unable to ride. Every cloud, and all that.

Her next clumsy act defies all belief at the level of violent self-destruction. This time it was Christmas Eve (what is it with her and the day before a special day? I'm surprised she wasn't bubble-wrapped on the day before the wedding). She was attempting to strap some lagging to the pipe for the outside tap on the stable block but, in her usual stubborn "I can manage" way, had neither the assistance she needed nor the right tools for the job. She is also, at times, too strong (or just heavy-handed) for her own good, as she demonstrated to perfection on this occasion. Tugging with all her strength on a chain that she would not admit was too short to go round the pipe, plus the post it was attached to, and the lagging too, she finally gave it one mighty tug… and snapped the thick – but rotten – wooden post clean in two which then smacked her with her own continued full force, straight between her eyes.

When she had quite finished staggering about, feeling a bit of an idiot (only a bit?), she also then felt the blood running down her face and, realising there was no hiding this one from the fiancé, went in the house to "surprise" the poor man with his new-look bride-to-be. She had managed to break her own nose, given herself what developed into a mightily impressive black eye and a really nasty head wound. Typically, she still didn't go to hospital, though if she'd realised the scar she'd be left with she might have made more effort, because – you guessed it – this wasn't the first time she'd broken her nose.

Again, the first time she had equine assistance. Soli this time. They had been show jumping at an indoor competition and were in the jump-off. The frighteningly quick Soli was uber-excited and on spotting her next fence just launched at it from a mile off, landed *on* the spread fence, sending poles flying, she fell and my human was thrown face-first into the dirt. Soli leapt up and trotted jauntily (and soundly) away while my human, somewhat less jauntily, managed to just about sit up before the St John's first aider came running over.

Now he was a gentleman of advancing years and my human, at that time, was a wee bairn (see, I'm picking up the Scottish lingo) in her early twenties, so it was with a twinkle in his eye that his first words to her were, "Right get your jodhs off, love" (pretty sure he wouldn't get away with that approach these days), despite there being clearly no injuries to her from the neck down. She just grinned, spat out the dirt she'd collected upon landing face-first, got a little shakily to her feet and remounted, jumped the rebuilt jump and a triple but then couldn't remember the rest of the course so had to retire.

On leaving the arena she spotted a couple of friends of hers, who had seen the whole thing, and said, "Oh hi, Sue, hi, Chris – didn't know you were coming," at which point they quietly told her to dismount, give them Soli and go and sit down. Turns out they had brought Soli and my human to the competition in their lorry, but she was concussed and had no recollection of that whatsoever! A revisit to the lovely St John's gentleman (jodhpurs remaining firmly on) confirmed concussion and a broken nose and that she should go to hospital to be checked over. Did she go? Did she heck.

In fact, the only time she did voluntarily take herself off to hospital (apparently being scraped off the floor by the ambulance men after Rubbish squished her doesn't count as voluntary because *she* didn't phone for the ambulance) was the only other time Soli fell. This time it was at a hunter trial. They had successfully completed the Novice course and were storming round the Open when, on approaching the stile fence at her usual alarming speed, Soli didn't notice an additional higher rail had been inserted for the Open class, so she clobbered it and it brought her down. Once again, that insane pony jumped back up and proceeded to show off a pretty flashy (and, yes, sound) trot across the field and back to the lorries, while my human failed this time to even make it to an upright position. She had damaged her knee (wrecked the ligaments, it turned out) and just couldn't move the joint at all. She was removed from the course by St John's Ambulance (good old St John's again!) and this time her jodhs legitimately did have to come off because her knee was already swelling up to football proportions.

Even she could see that she couldn't shrug off this one and her friend kindly drove her to hospital. Unfortunately, my human's response to pain is often, bizarrely, to get a bit giggly (must be some sort of hysteria) and her mate didn't exactly help, as she found it hilarious struggling to half carry my hopping floppy-from-laughter human into A&E. So much snorting and giggling did nothing to help get her seen quickly and it was many hours later a somewhat more meek human was wrapped up in an attractive Tubigrip arrangement and sent home for rest and elevation. So that was her back to commuting to work the next day then.

Soli was, as ever, absolutely fine. The only time that tough little mare was beaten by injury was as a six-year-old when she was kicked by a small unshod pony. It fractured her cannon bone and fractured her shoulder too. It was touch and go whether she'd survive both injuries, let alone ever be sound enough to ride, but after months of box rest and in-hand "walking" (zebedee on ecstasy at the end of a lead rope), that amazing pony was declared sound and remained so for another twenty-five very active years.

The Big Day
(and the Day After)

So it was pretty miraculous that my clumsy, accident-prone human made it to their wedding day sound enough to pass a trot-up and with none of the sort of blemishes that would have her forcibly removed from a show ring.

In the preceding weeks she had given much thought to the most important element of the wedding, i.e. how I could be involved. For some reason the fiancé had chosen SWMBO as his best man instead of me, which must have been an oversight. The dogs had already been appointed ring-bearers, so that position was thankfully gone (I couldn't bear the responsibility), plus I refused to wear a kilt or even the "splash of tartan" dress code (with my colouring, was she mad?). She had thought about getting us horses all bathed and plaited and our manes decorated with blue ribbons in harmony with the flowers and decorations she had ordered for the marquee (I *knew* she was matchy-matchy at heart). This I thoroughly approved of, but for some reason she decided she wouldn't want to spend the entire morning before her 1.15pm ceremony knee deep in horse shampoo and fiddly plaiting ribbons, instead having her own hair done, rather selfishly.

It was decided, therefore, that BB and I would attend au naturel, by virtue of being turned out in the field beside the marquee. The thinking being that our natural curiosity would bring us close by, to attend without the risk of anyone's pristine wedding outfit getting covered in green slobber, or white hair if BB decided someone was the perfect size for him to use as a scratching post. This would offer plenty of charming photo opportunities while still keeping a (shiny new) post and rail fence between us.

This delightful image worked on the basis that the marquee would be erected two or three days before the wedding, to give them time to furnish and decorate it, just adding the flowers as a final flourish upon their delivery on the morning of the big day, and stocking it with posh nibbles and drink to sustain the guests. This timescale would also give BB and I a chance to get used to the marquee being there.

Inevitably this is not how matters unfolded.

The days before the wedding were too windy to erect a marquee and be confident that it wouldn't end up in the middle of the firth if left unattended for a few hours, let alone overnight. And so, to my human's utter horror, its erection, furnishing and decoration all had to be left until just a few hours before the ceremony. This did not fill her with confidence or happy thoughts. Thankfully, her younger sister, a wedding photographer by trade, who had, therefore, been to a wedding or two in her time, worked some very quick magic with the mini army of family and friends, and the result was even better than my human had imagined.

However, us horses were less impressed. One minute we were grazing peacefully and the next there was a flurry of vehicles and activity and a monstrous white flapping spaceship appeared. A brief lull in activities was followed by a procession of smartly dressed (with the compulsory splashes of tartan) guests, and then a bagpiper noisily leading my human in a strange long white dress and footwear that looked highly inappropriate for walking across fields, and her mum to the spaceship.

Well, BB and I needed to see no more. It all looked like the kind of thing sensible horses should stay well away from. So, for the entire ceremony, we remained firmly at the furthest corner of the field so any photo opportunities would only be available to those armed with the sort of camera equipment David Attenborough's team take on safari.

We didn't get away from the whole shenanigans completely, though.

The next day, after they had all returned from the castle hotel do, some a little worse for wear, they were apparently all huddled round their caffeine fixes when the sun popped out.

The wedding day itself had been a bit overcast, even drizzly at times, and neither the photographer sister nor the bride and groom had quite got the outdoors images they had hoped for. So they decided to re-enact it and have a Wedding Take Two.

The bride and groom donned their respective dress and kilt outfits once more and headed for the beach, with the dogs too, and got some amazing photos. Of course, not being the wedding day proper, my human not only didn't have to worry if her dress got sandy or wet at the bottom but she even had appropriate footwear – by some happy coincidence one of her wedding gifts from her colleagues at work, who clearly knew her so well, had been a pair of dinky white welly boots, complete with fancy decoration, which stood her in excellent stead for wading into the water on the beach and then to come to our field and finally get those all-important photos with the real best man – me.

It's All About Me

Finally, life settled down.

My human, no longer distracted by insignificant little matters like renovating houses and organising a wedding, could finally focus on the most important person in her life – me. I was now fit and well, and I had my little buddy BB to help take the strain if she got all keen and decided to ride every day.

Happily, her opinion of riding in anything other than nice weather is the same as mine – we just don't see the point. Neither of us enjoys it; neither of us wants to school with gritted teeth or a hunched back against the rain, and where's the pleasure in riding along the beach when you can't lift your head to admire the view because of the sting of the wind-lashed hail on your face? Nope, at those moments we have "quality time" – my favourite – with grooming and scratching aplenty.

At last, she planned to get me back out to some dressage competitions. I do still love a pony party and hadn't been out with her for three years, so I was thrilled when we started practising our centre lines again. I like nothing more than steaming down the centre line in my biggest trot and hand-braking to a banging square halt just as the judge's eyes are starting to widen in alarm.

We were relieved to discover that there are two venues which run affiliated shows that are only about forty-five minutes away. The first we went to, which my human had been warned by several people had an arena that could ride "a little deep", was friendly and the class sizes small, so not an intimidating first Scottish outing.

Apart from the presence of a pretty ferocious-looking Shetland in the field beside the warm-up, I warmed up like the pro I am, as if the three-year gap had been only three weeks, and my human and I were looking forward to showing our best work in the tests.

Turns out they weren't kidding about the "a little deep" warning. I stepped into the arena, picked up trot and my human wondered if a leg had dropped off. I was all over the place. I really don't do "deep" and I barely do "soft" – I'm a good-to-firm man.

As opposed to the legendary Rubbish, who, being 7/8 thoroughbred and that all-important 1/8 Irish bog pony, loved a bit of deep going; in fact, the softer the better for him. Once my human jumped him at Hickstead when the ground was (in my opinion) appalling. She was prepared for it when they towed the lorries *into* the lorry park fields through the mud, never mind trying to get them out. By the time she got to the warm-up it was carnage – a bottomless sea of mud. The course itself looked better... marginally. And so, not to risk him in the warm-up, she just trotted a bit, slopped over a cross pole and then they went in and jumped their round, one round against the clock. Rubbish loved it. He romped round clear and quick for the team and looked as smug as it is possible for a horse to look when he came out of the ring.

I am not Rubbish, in any sense.

Back in the bottomless dressage arena, my human all but carried me around my two tests. All our practising and training went completely out of the window and each test just felt like five minutes of survival, struggling to maintain the correct pace, let alone even considering bend, suppleness, engagement, balance, etc., etc. I have to confess I may have fallen "a little" behind the leg at times and we both finished each test huffing and puffing and wobbly-legged.

We still won both classes, though! Does it count as a win when there's only us and one other combination in each class? I'm going to say yes – yes, it does. A red rosette is a red rosette, after all!

We tried the other venue a few weeks later and found it even friendlier, with a surface much more to my liking. We put on a much better show, and again won both classes. When I saw my human return to the trailer with two red rosettes and a grin a mile wide, I think I could have given a post-muddy-romp-at-Hickstead Rubbish a run for his money in the smugness stakes.

Later that season, after my human had pushed us both at home in our training, she finally braved entering two Medium tests, a level at which we had only once competed, several years ago when we managed a mediocre score.

She was nervous. We hadn't managed to have any training since the move to Scotland so had no idea if all our work was getting us in the right direction, plus I'd had my spine surgery and we were both a few years older and less supple… She feared she was pushing me a step too far.

So it was with nervous excitement that we rode our two Medium tests. And even more nervous excitement that she awaited the results. She couldn't quite believe it when they were announced. Not only had we won both classes, we had achieved scores the like of which we hadn't seen since our Prelim days! And in doing so had qualified for the Area Festival!

I was back in sash territory at last.